The Truth About

ISLAM &
WOMEN

John Ankerberg
Emir Caner

HARVEST HOUSE PUBLISHERS

EUGENE, OREGON

Cover by Dugan Design Group, Bloomington, Minnesota

Cover photos © Roberto A. Sanchez / iStockphoto; StockXpert

THE TRUTH ABOUT ISLAM AND WOMEN
The Truth About Islam Series
Copyright © 2009 by John Ankerberg and Emir Caner
Published by Harvest House Publishers
Eugene, Oregon 97402
www.harvesthousepublishers.com

Library of Congress Cataloging-in-Publication Data
    Ankerberg, John, 1945-
    The truth about Islam and women / John Ankerberg and Emir Caner.
       p. cm.
    Includes bibliographical references.
    ISBN 978-0-7369-2503-7 (pbk.)
    1. Women in Islam. 2. Islam—Controversial literature. 3. Apologetics. 4 Christianity and other religions—Islam. 5. Islam—Relations—Christianity. I. Caner, Emir Fethi. II. Title.
    BP173.4.A54 2009
    297.082—dc22

                                                                    2008038178

Printed in the United States of America

09 10 11 12 13 14 15 16 17 / VP-SK / 10 9 8 7 6 5 4 3 2 1

Contents

Section Four
Women and Family

Section Five
Women and Society

Section Six
Women and Infidelity

Section Seven
Women and Jesus

Why the Truth Matters

On a hot July summer morning, Omar and Aisha rush to the local hospital in Damascus, Syria, in eager anticipation of the birth of their first child. Dreaming of this day for years, they were preparing long before Aisha ever found out she was with child. As is common for many Muslim women, Aisha prayed to Allah about her desires to be a mother while repeatedly reciting sura 103 (*Al-Asr,* "the Declining Day") and sura 112 (*Al-Ikhlas,* "Sincerity").[1]

Omar, too, frequently recited sura 12 (*Yusuf,* "Joseph") in hope that Allah would give them a beautiful child. After notification of her pregnancy, Aisha sought to perform good works, repented of prior sins (*taubat*), and prayed during the early hours of the day, three activities many Muslims believe are necessary in order to have healthy children. During her prenatal period, Aisha nourished her unborn child with *halal* (permitted) food. Muhammad once explained, "If a woman eats sweet melon, she will give birth to a handsome and pretty child." These two devout Muslims diligently followed Islamic customs, hoping that Allah will bless their family with many children.

Then, a baby girl is born. This beautiful, brown-eyed, seven-pound-nine-ounce infant has entered the world of Islam, a world intended to be a cradle-to-the-grave religion in which there are no irreligious acts. Immediately, her father whispers into her right ear *Allahu Akbar* ("God is Great"), an act intended to protect the little one from the wiles of Satan. He proceeds to whisper the rest of the call to prayer in her left ear.

The baby is brought home as the excited young parents gleefully relate the news to their friends and family. On the seventh day after her birth, Omar sacrifices an animal (*aqiqah*) in proper manner. He ensures the goat is free from obvious handicap and sickness.[2] Like her mother and father, who were named after stalwarts of the Islamic faith, the baby is given a very precious name—Amina—the name of the prophet Muhammad's own mother, who died while he was still a young child.[3] Amina is brought to a respected man in the community, who places softened dates in her mouth (*tahneek*), a ritual whose significance is only known to Allah and Muhammad.[4] Today, the joy of new creation is celebrated by the entire community that surrounds this little one.

Amina's life will be much like her birth. Her devoted Muslim parents will strictly follow the dictates of the Qur'an and the *Sunnah* (the example of Muhammad[5]) as they raise her and all subsequent children with which they are blessed. As a female, her life will strictly conform to the commands found within the revelation of Allah. As a child, the daughter will be educated in the basics of Islamic theology, its five pillars and six fundamental beliefs.[6] She will learn about the "Seal of the Prophets" (sura 33:40), Muhammad, and Muhammad's daughter Fatima.

> In submitting herself to Allah and doing what is right according to the Qur'an, she hopes that one day Allah will be pleased and grant her Paradise.

In addition, she will be taught what to say when she wakes up in the morning, how to greet those along the way, and how to pray five times daily. Modesty will be her life lesson, from the way she dresses to her demeanor in public. The Qur'an will stipulate her rights in life, marriage, and work, with the ultimate goal that she herself will one day take on the greatest task she can have in this life—motherhood. In submitting herself to Allah and doing what is right according to the Qur'an, she hopes that one day Allah will be pleased and grant her Paradise.

Come and explore the fate of the women of Islam, a journey tens of millions of women have taken during the past 14 centuries.[7] From birth to death, from creation to eternity, from family to society, walk the path of Islam and its impact on women. Along the way, you will not only gain an understanding of Islam, you will also see the stark differences between the values of Islam and of Christianity.

The Truth About Islam and Women gives the essentials of what the second-largest religion in the world declares about the female sex. But don't simply study the facts. Understand the repercussions these beliefs have on the lives of countless female babies born at local hospitals around the Muslim world each day, including many born today in North America. And remember, for us it is a study—for women born into Islam, it is life.

A Guide to Arabic
Terms and Abbreviations

Though many of the Arabic words used in this book are described in their context, a few foundational terms are noted here to help explain what you may encounter in these pages. The version of the Qur'an used in this book, unless otherwise indicated, is the translation of Yusuf Ali,* considered one of the most authoritative versions among English-speaking Muslims.

Bukhari: Named after its compiler, this *Hadith* (tradition) is the most respected compilation of Muhammad's words and deeds, also known as the *Sunna*.

Dawud: One of the six collections of the words and deeds of Muhammad, this collection of traditions, or reports (ahadith) focuses on law.

Caliph (also *calif*): The title of Islamic leaders after Muhammad's death. Among the Shiites, caliphs have been replaced by *imams*.

Five Pillars: The five foundational spiritual practices in Islam required of all Muslims in order to enter Paradise (see question 11).

Hadith: "Story": collection of sayings and examples of Muhammad; highest Islamic authority after the Qur'an.

Hajj: One of the five pillars of Islam, which commands all Muslims

---

* Abdullah Yusuf Ali, tr., *The Holy Quran*. Quotations marked MGQ are from Mohammed Marmaduke Pickthall, *The Meaning of the Glorious Quran*.

able to do so to visit the Muslim holy site in Mecca at least once during their lifetime.

Imam: A Muslim holy leader, usually in charge of a local mosque. In Shiite Islam, a supreme spiritual guide who is a direct descendant of Ali, and thus Muhammad.

Jihad: An Arabic term for "resistance," interpreted as a spiritual struggle or as an external struggle (violence and war).

Mecca: Islam's most holy site, which all able Muslims must visit at least once during their lifetime.

Mosque: A building in which Muslims hold prayers and worship activities.

Muslim: One of the most respected (*sahih*) compilations of the words and deeds of Muhammad, this collection, named for its compiler, contains about 4000 traditions (*ahadith*).

Qur'an: The holy book of Muslims, said to contain, word for word, the instruction Allah gave to Muhammad, the founder of Islam.

Shia: Literally, "faction." *Shiite* has come to mean a "follower of Ali"—one who believes the caliph Ali was the true successor to Muhammad.

Sunni: "People of the Way." Followers of Abu Bakr and Umar, the first two caliphs, as successors to Muhammad.

Sura (sometimes *surah*): The name used for each section of the Qur'an; equivalent to "chapters" in reference to the Bible.

Influential Women in the Life of Muhammad

*Beautified for mankind is love of the joys (that come) from women and offspring; and stored-up heaps of gold and silver, and horses branded (with their mark), and cattle and land. That is comfort of the life of the world. Allah! With Him is a more excellent abode.**

—SURA 3:14 MGQ

1

Did Muhammad liberate or enslave women?

In today's society, Muslims go to great lengths to proclaim Muhammad as the liberator and protector of women. He was the one Allah commanded to say, "O mankind! Lo, I am the messenger of Allah to you all" (7:158). Therefore, they assert that his wisdom and insight far exceeded that of his contemporaries. As such, it demonstrated clearly to all that his knowledge came from divine inspiration. Islamic scholars repeatedly argue that before Muhammad's political and religious ascension, females had few, if any, rights within the Arabian Peninsula, and their lives were deemed inconsequential.

Professor of Islamic studies Haifaa Jawad suggests that women in pre-Islamic times

> were viewed as the embodiment of sin, misfortune, disgrace and shame, and they had no rights or position in society

---

* In quotations from the Qur'an in this book, parentheses were added by the translator. Brackets indicate explanations inserted by the authors of this book.

whatsoever...However, in the Arabian peninsula (the birth-place of Islam), the situation of women prior to Islam was markedly worse...They were treated as sex objects with no respect at all for their dignity.[8]

Muhammad, Muslims say, changed everything and gave women their true divine right of dignity and worth. He granted women inheritance rights, something foreign to Western thought until two centuries ago. The most notable example of Muhammad's liberation of women was the elimination of the heinous act of female infanticide. Before Islam, pagan Arabs, in need of males to fight in the battle for survival, would murder female infants because they placed an undue burden upon their tribe.[9]

The Qur'an explicitly condemns such an act:

> When news is brought to one of them, of (the birth of) a female (child), his face darkens, and he is filled with inward grief! With shame does he hide himself from his people, because of the bad news he has had! Shall he retain it on (sufferance and) contempt, or bury it in the dust? Ah! What an evil (choice) they decide on? (16:58-59 MGQ).[10]

But upon further review of pre-Islamic history, questions arise as to Muhammad's emancipation of women. True, Islam must be credited for eradicating female infanticide on the Arabian Peninsula, but apparently the practice was actually quite rare and was religious in origin.[11] Additionally, even though Islam grants women inheritance rights, women are given only *half* the share of a man. Even these monies are not fully in her control.[12] The freedoms pagan Arab women enjoyed were many times greater than after Islam conquered the region. For example:

- Before Islamic law, women were permitted to have more than one husband (polyandry).

- Pre-Islamic rules granted women the right to live a life that

was "neither cloistered nor veiled" and was not segregated
by sex.

- If physically abused or poorly treated, women could migrate
  to another tribe.

- Before Islam, women enjoyed great political power and took
  an integral part in decisions of society such as military nego-
  tiations and alliances.[13]

In reality, outside of the atrocious act of infanticide, women were
actually worse off after the advent of Islam. One meaningful way to
illustrate this is to take a glimpse into the lives of the most influential
women in Muhammad's life. In the end, it is easy to see that the more
Islam gained in prominence, the less women were given their proper
respect.

2

What about Muhammad's mother?

*A man came to Allah's Apostle and said, "O Allah's Apostle! Who
is more entitled to be treated with the best companionship by me?"
The Prophet said, "Your mother." The man said, "Who is next?"
The Prophet said, "Your mother." The man further said, "Who is
next?" The Prophet said. "Your mother." The man asked for the
fourth time, "Who is next?" The Prophet said, "Your father."*

—Bukhari 8.2

Muhammad's childhood is fraught with sad events, including the
death of his father, Abdullah, before his birth, and the death of his
mother when he was just six years old. In fact, Muhammad spent little
time with his mother, Amina, even during those six years, since it was
customary for an infant to be given to a wet nurse for at least two years.
The nurse would breast-feed the child and provide a safer and healthier

environment in the desert than the city of Mecca offered. In the case of Muhammad, most of the Bedouin nurses rejected him "because we hoped to get payment from the child's father."[14]

Finally, a poor woman, Halima, decided to nurse him, hoping that "God will bless us on his account."[15] It is said that Halima and her husband were bequeathed great blessings, such as an abundance of milk from their once parched animals, though others had not a drop due to dry conditions and lack of rain. After two years, blessed with such great fortune, Halima requested that Muhammad stay with her for another two years. Amina, Muhammad's mother, readily agreed, due in part to disease that was ravaging parts of the Meccan community.

Muhammad later returned to his mother and enjoyed a short time with her. But when Amina took her son to Medina to show him where his father was buried, on the return trip she fell ill and died. Muhammad, who "must have first learned what it means to be an orphan"[16] while hearing the story of his father, returned to Mecca twice orphaned.

Ironically, Muhammad's childhood may be best summed up in one word: *unnoticed*. The Qur'an and Hadith say little of it. Indeed, outside of a biography written more than 140 years after Muhammad's death, which attempts to portray the importance of the prophet even as a child, it seems the supposed greatness of Muhammad was not detected by those surrounding him during his early years.

As one author noted,

> Having failed to suspect the future greatness of this obscure Qurayshite [the prominent Arabian tribe to which Muhammad belonged], no one had bothered to observe him, still less preserve the impressions collected.[17]

The Qur'an gives significant insight into Muhammad's psyche when it says, "Did [Allah] not find you an orphan and give you shelter (and care)? And He found you wandering, and He gave you guidance. And He found you in need, and made you independent" (sura 93:6-8).

3

What about Muhammad's first wife, Khadijah?

And covet not the thing in which Allah hath made some of
you excel others. Unto men a fortune from that which they
have earned, and unto women a fortune from that which
they have earned. (Envy not one another) but ask Allah of
His bounty. Lo! Allah is ever Knower of all things.

—SURA 4:32 MGQ

As respected Qur'an commentator Yusuf Ali argues, Muhammad's independence (sura 93:8) was granted in the person of his first wife, Khadijah, who "not only raised him above want, but made him independent of worldly needs in his later life, enabling him to devote his whole time to the service of Allah."[18]

Khadijah, a wealthy merchant woman twice widowed, hired Muhammad to lead a caravan to Syria and trade on her behalf. Muhammad, highly successful and intensely loyal, impressed his employer, who shortly thereafter asked him if he would be interested in uniting in marriage.[19]

The 25-year-old Muhammad and Khadijah, at age 40, quickly began a family, which eventually consisted of two sons and four daughters. All four daughters survived to adulthood, but the two sons died in childhood.[20] Khadijah, necessarily obedient to her husband, managed the growing household while at the same time supervising the family business. Muhammad was free to pursue a life of meditation which, by the time he was 40 years old, led to revelations from Allah. Khadijah became his greatest supporter and first convert to Islam. After 25 years of marriage, she passed away. Until Muhammad was 50 years old, he had only known one woman.

> Muhammad had a skewed view of women's intellect and considered them "deficient in intelligence."

In many ways Khadijah personifies the transition between pre-Islamic and post-Islamic culture. Here was a powerful woman who, before the advent of Islam, chose her own path and ran her own business. She pursued Muhammad, supervised men and, due to her wealth, was considered a leader within the community.

This, of course, is a far cry from the arranged marriages of Islam, in which a woman's silence is considered full consent (Bukhari 9.79). Even though Khadijah was Muhammad's encourager when he questioned the revelation he received in the cave (Bukhari 1.1-3), Muhammad had a skewed view of women's intellect and considered them "deficient in intelligence" (Bukhari 1.301).

Khadijah was a woman whose wealth gave her social freedom, yet Islam initiated the existence of the cloistered woman, whose social interaction is extremely limited. When women are in public, they must "lower their gaze," they "should not display their beauty," and they must "draw their veils" (sura 24:31). Today this is typically interpreted as meaning that women are limited in their social interaction. They are relegated to a more private life, victims of a culture that views their freedom as potentially dangerous to the community.

In today's Islamic world, it would be highly unlikely that Muhammad would have ever met, much less married, Khadijah.

4

What about Muhammad's later marriages?

Narrated Aisha:

that the Prophet married her when she was six years old and he consummated his marriage when she was nine years old, and then she remained with him for nine years (that is, till his death).

—BUKHARI 7.64

Desiring companionship with many women after Khadijah's death,

Muhammad entered a time of polygamy and sensuality. He married nearly a dozen women, far greater than the maximum allowed by the Qur'an (sura 4:3). According to Muhammad, he received a special revelation from Allah that granted him permission to marry as many women as he chose:

> O Prophet! We have made lawful to thee thy wives to whom thou hast paid their dowers; and those whom thy right hand possesses out of the captives of war whom Allah has assigned to thee (sura 33:50).

Muhammad's sexual prowess was widely known and proudly documented in the Hadith, which records,

> The Prophet used to visit all his wives in a round, during the day and night and they were eleven in number. I asked Anas, "Had the Prophet the strength for it?" Anas replied, "We used to say that the Prophet was given the strength of thirty (men)" (Bukhari 5.268).

And, as one Christian author points out, "Slaves, captives, and concubines represent another category, which is numerically impossible to document."[21]

It seems Muhammad enjoyed any and all pleasures he desired, as indicated in the following tradition: "Any of the female slaves of Medina could take hold of the hand of Allah's Apostle and take him wherever they wished" (Bukhari 8.97).[22] Yet the one relationship which to this day garners the most attention was Muhammad's marriage to Aisha, the young daughter of one of his earliest and most loyal followers, Abu Bakr. As the authoritative words of Islamic tradition above illustrate, Muhammad began intimate relations with the girl when she was *only nine years old.* She was, in fact, the only woman Muhammad married that was a virgin.

Islamic scholars do their very best to justify this unconscionable action. Some scholars assert that Aisha was unaware of the implications of marriage until she reached puberty.[23] Other scholars attempt to revise her age.[24] Still other Muslims simply argue that she reached puberty quite young and therefore was physiologically capable of such interaction with Muhammad.[25]

The consequences of this arrangement still haunt many Muslim women today. In countries such as Yemen, there is no age limit as to when a girl can be given to a man. Girls are often pressured by their parents to consent to early marriages and are forced to follow a custom of Islam that dates back to its founder.[26]

5

What other controversy about marriage stems from the life of Muhammad?

Then when Zaid had dissolved (his marriage) with [Zaynab]…We joined her in marriage to [Muhammad]: in order that (in future) there may be no difficulty to the Believers in (the matter of) marriage with the wives of their adopted sons, when the latter have dissolved… (their marriage) with them. And Allah's command must be fulfilled.

—SURA 33:37

Zaid was a slave turned adopted son of Muhammad, who converted to Islam very early in the movement. He was married to Zaynab, the cousin of Muhammad and daughter of Abd al-Mutalib, the uncle of the prophet. Reports indicate that the marriage was a miserable one and that Zaid wished to divorce his wife. Historians further affirm that Zaynab was terribly unhappy with her husband as well and had intended to marry the prophet from the very beginning. Muhammad, uncomfortable with the thought of taking his daughter-in-law, first disregarded any such thought until, as seen in the verse above, he received another special revelation from Allah, permitting him to marry his son's ex-wife. The revelation found the union acceptable since Zaid was his adopted son and not his biological child.

The story, however, is far more about Muhammad's lust for a young, beautiful woman. On a day when Zaid was not at home, Muhammad visited Zaynab and was obviously struck by her beauty. He related, "Gracious Lord! Good Heavens! How you do turn the hearts of men!"[27] When Zaynab notified her husband of the prophet's words, Zaid, out of intense loyalty and devotion, immediately offered to divorce his wife. Zaynab was smitten with the idea herself and, except for public opinion, which would look at such a union as incestuous, apparently would not have thought twice before marrying Muhammad. But with his new revelation, the taboo was removed. Nonetheless, even Aisha was stunned at the quick change of cultural norms and exclaimed, "It seems to me that your Lord hastens to satisfy your desire."[28]

Muhammad's legacy is absolutely clear as one honestly and critically looks into the intimate life of the prophet. First, rules for his marriages were uniquely revealed to him, prohibiting Muslims from following his life too closely. Second, his relationship with the young girl Aisha has led to the odious tradition that Muslim girls are ready for marriage at an all-too-young age. Third, it seems his marriages reveal that formative Islam and its revelations were far more concerned about Muhammad's happiness than the well-being of others—in particular, women.

For example, Muhammad was so incensed at his harem at one point that he abandoned them for a month and threatened to divorce every one of them. The women were put in their place, and Muhammad remained united to all of them. The Qur'an records this dire warning to his wives:

> O Prophet! Why have you forbidden yourself that which God has made lawful unto you?...Verily God has sanctioned the revocation of your oaths...
> If [Muhammad] divorces you, God will give him in your stead wives more submissive unto God, believers, pious,

repentant, devout, fasting; both women married previously,
and virgins.[29]

In the end, a woman's place in Islam is largely determined by the
selfish sensualities and insatiable desires of a man who lived 14 centuries
ago.

Women in the Creation Order

6

How does Islam misunderstand the biblical concept of the creation of women?

O ye Children of Adam! Let not Satan seduce you, in the same manner as he got your parents out of the Garden, stripping them of their raiment, to expose their shame: for he and his tribe see you from a position where ye cannot see them: we made the Satans friends (only) to those without faith.

—SURA 7:27

Muslim scholars regularly contend that the biblical account of the Fall in Genesis 3 has led to countless centuries of the denigration of women. In blaming Eve for the introduction of sin into the human race, Jews and Christians have communicated a highly imbalanced and perverted view of women which, until the advent of Islam, brought unfair blame and untold suffering.

One Muslim author argues,

> To rehabilitate the status of women in society, Islam denounced the old myth of Eve as temptress and source of evil, as the cause of original sin and the fall of humankind. According to the Qur'an the woman is not responsible for Adam's first mistake: both were equally wrong in disobeying God.[1]

Muslims maintain that there is full equality and responsibility among the couple in both obedience and disobedience.

However, the argument used by Muslims fails to truly address the biblical record. First, the Genesis account clearly indicates that both Adam and Eve took of the fruit and were responsible for the consequences (3:6). Additionally, the narrative places greater blame on Adam since God sought him out first (3:9); moreover, the directive to not eat the fruit was given to him *before* Eve was even created (2:15-17). Adam, as spiritual leader of the home (implied in 3:17), was accountable for his actions and the lack of protection he provided to his wife.

More significant, death came through Adam (3:19). This is supported by the New Testament as well. Romans 5:12 tells of how "sin entered the world through one man, and death through sin, and in this way death came to all men, because all sinned." Death entered the world through Adam's sin, and is removed from this world only by the Second Adam, our sin-bearer Jesus Christ (Isaiah 53:12; 1 Peter 2:24).

Since Muslims are unwilling to accept the Bible's explanation of humanity's Fall, they consequently reject the solution found in the person of Jesus Christ. Keep firmly in mind that the Islamic view of creation is inseparable from their view of salvation (guidance). Thus, Islam does not teach that men and women are lost (see Luke 15:1-7), and therefore Muslims do not seek to be saved (see, in contrast, Acts 2:40). As proclaimed in sura 7:27, all men, all women, are solely responsible for their own sins and, if God wills (sura 14:4), [2] for their own salvation.

The problem Islam refuses to recognize

Islam does not recognize the seriousness of sin, nor our inability to turn away the wrath of a holy and just God over that sin. The prophet Isaiah outlines the problem: "Your iniquities have separated you from your God; your sins have hidden his face from you, so that he will not hear" (Isaiah 59:2).

Jesus affirms that sin separates mankind from God, also making clear his claim to be God himself: "I told you that you would die in your sins; if you do not believe that I am the one I claim to be, you will indeed die in your sins" (John 8:24). And Paul explains, "All have sinned and fall short of the glory of God" (Romans 3:23).

Further, Islam does not realize that a perfect righteousness from God can be obtained by sinners when they put their ultimate trust in Jesus as their sin-bearer. Jesus is the one who made payment for the sins of the world that was accepted by God.

The words Paul wrote to the Jews can be equally applied to Muslims: "Since they did not know the righteousness that comes from God and sought to establish their own, they did not submit to God's righteousness" (Romans 10:3). But the Bible tells us God's full acceptance comes only from him:

- "Now a righteousness from God, apart from [keeping the] law, has been made known...This righteousness [perfect standing before God] from God [not ourselves] comes through faith in Jesus Christ to all who believe. There is no difference, for all have sinned" (Romans 3:21-23).

- "We maintain that a man is justified by faith apart from observing the law" (Romans 3:28).

- Jesus declared, "My Father's will is that everyone who looks to the Son and believes in him shall have eternal life, and I will raise him up at the last day" (John 6:40). He also said, "Whoever believes in the Son has eternal life, but whoever rejects the Son will not see life, for God's wrath remains on him" (John 3:36).

Though God's righteousness declares that "the wages of sin is death," as we have already seen, he has also provided the needed righteousness: "The free gift of God is eternal life in Christ Jesus our Lord" (Romans 6:23 NASB).

How does a person obtain the free gift of God, which is eternal life—his life in us now and in heaven—and God's cleansing of all our sins? The Bible provides clear direction:

- Peter writes of Jesus that "He Himself bore our sins in His body on the cross" (1 Peter 2:24 NASB).

- Paul tells us that God "has rescued us from the dominion of darkness and brought us into the kingdom of the Son he loves, in whom we have redemption, the forgiveness of sins" (Colossians 1:13-14).

- Jesus himself said, "I give them eternal life, and they shall never perish; no one can snatch them out of my hand" (John 10:28).

In sum, by removing depravity from mankind, Islam also discards the salvation of God provided through faith in Jesus Christ. Perhaps this stark contrast between the two largest religions in the world can be seen best within their sacred texts. The Qur'an declares, "Nor can a bearer of burdens bear another's burden. If one heavily laden should call another to (bear) his load, not the least portion of it can be carried (by the other)" (sura 35:18).

In contrast, Jesus comforted others with these words: "Come to Me, all who are weary and heavy-laden, and I will give you rest" (Matthew 11:28 NASB). Not only does Christianity have a greater regard for women's well-being on earth—it also provides both women and men all that is needed for eternal life.

7

What is a woman's essential being and purpose?

And behold, We said: "O Adam! Dwell thou and thy wife in the Garden; and eat of the bountiful things therein as (where and when) ye will; but approach not this tree, or ye run into harm and transgression."

—SURA 2:35

Ironically, Eve is never actually named in the Qur'an. The Hadiths, however, include a few sparse references to her. A Christian must realize that the greatest difference between the creation of woman in the biblical narrative from the account of the Qur'an is that the Bible declares woman is formed in the image of God.

Genesis 5:1-2 reports, "When God created man, he made him in the likeness of God. He created them male and female and blessed them. And when they were created, he called them 'man.'" This emphasis cannot be underestimated. Men and women alike are to "rule over" all the earth and every animal (Genesis 1:26). Woman's spiritual nature is representative of God's nature, indicating she is of supreme value and worth. She was created in deepest essence—mind, emotion, and will—to be in fellowship with her Creator.

As one Christian theologian pointed out, "We belong to God… Commitment, devotion, love, loyalty, service to God—all of these are proper responses for those who bear the image of God."[3] Thus, Christianity places great importance on a woman's individual responsibility and liberty before God, while Islam stresses God's sovereignty and will presiding over a woman's life. One commentator explained it this way:

> So great is God that in the Islamic view He overpowers human liberty. This suggests a kind of determinism. What God knows and does is eternal and necessary and can't be changed, and no individual will, no knowledge of singulars or contingency, is possible to God. He doesn't concern himself with things like us, and you can't talk about human beings as images of God.[4]

For a woman to say she was created in God's image amounts to the highest sin in Islam, *shirk*—partnering something or someone with God. For Muslims, God's greatness cannot be compromised by such doctrine, and his glory will not be shared with anyone. Such a belief marks the advocate as an infidel, an unbeliever who has succumbed to the wiles of the devil and, as such, is deserving of God's worst punishment.[5]

8

Was Eve's salvation linked to Adam?

Lo! men who surrender unto Allah, and women who surrender, and men who believe and women who believe, and men who

> *obey and women who obey, and men who speak the truth and*
> *women who speak the truth, and men who persevere (in righteous-*
> *ness) and women who persevere, and men who are humble and*
> *women who are humble, and men who give alms and women who*
> *give alms, and men who fast and women who fast, and men who*
> *guard their modesty and women who guard (their modesty), and*
> *men who remember Allah much and women who remember—*
> *Allah hath prepared for them forgiveness and a vast reward.*
>
> —SURA 33:35[6] MGQ

At first glance, the above verse from the Qur'an seems to indicate that women have an equal obligation in spiritual things,[7] and an equal opportunity for forgiveness and reward. They are mandated to believe and act correctly, just as men are. But upon more critical investigation, it becomes apparent that Eve's essential purpose in the Islamic view of creation is her intimate devotion to her husband (sura 7:189).

A woman's salvation is integrally linked to her husband, as one tradition pointedly warns:

> The Prophet said: "I was shown the Hell-fire and that the majority of its dwellers were women who were ungrateful." It was asked, "Do they disbelieve in Allah?" (or are they ungrateful to Allah?) He replied, "They are ungrateful to their husbands and are ungrateful for the favors and the good (charitable deeds) done to them. If you have always been good (benevolent) to one of them and then she sees something in you (not of her liking), she will say, 'I have never received any good from you'" (Bukhari 1.28).

One similar Hadith explicitly argues that women are, according to Muhammad, not just a "majority" in hell, but are "*most of the inhabitants*" (Bukhari 2.161, emphasis added). Even though the Qur'an teaches, "Whoever works righteousness, man or woman, and has Faith, verily, to him will We give life" (sura 16:97), the works a woman does are inseparable from her relationship to her husband.

In addition, a woman's disobedience to her husband is traced back to Eve and her disobedience. "The Prophet said, 'But for the Israelis, meat would not decay and but for Eve, wives would never betray their husbands'" (Bukhari 4.547).[8] Although Muslims adamantly argue that Christianity blames Eve for the sin in this world, it appears Muhammad blamed Eve for the heinous sin of ungratefulness, a sin that can, by itself, consign women to hell.

9

Was Eve genetically inferior?

Allah's Apostle said, "Treat women nicely, for a women is created from a rib, and the most curved portion of the rib is its upper portion, so, if you should try to straighten it, it will break, but if you leave it as it is, it will remain crooked. So treat women nicely."

—Bukhari 4.548[9]

Women, according to Islam, were created inferior to men, a weakness that is first and foremost seen in their physical limitations. Islamic sources abound with verses that consider women less able to fulfill their spiritual obligations and exempt them from religious requirements given to men. For example:

- Women are exempted from daily prayers and fasting during menstruation.

- They are exempted from daily prayers and fasting for 40 days after the birth of a child.

- Congregational prayers, mandatory to men, are optional for women due to their obligations as mothers.[10]

The most notorious example is Islam's discouragement of women's involvement in *jihad* (holy war). Instead, it is far better for women to fulfill the Hajj, the fifth Pillar of Islam, which requires all economically able Muslims to make the pilgrimage to Mecca. As one eyewitness remembered, "[Aisha] said, 'O Allah's Apostle! We consider Jihad as the best deed.' The Prophet said, 'The best Jihad (for women) is Hajj Mabrur'" (Bukhari 2.595).[11]

This inferiority is not confined to the physiological makeup of a woman in Islamic teachings, but to her mind as well. Her physical constraints, for example, directly relate to her mental prowess. A woman, according to Muhammad, is simply incapable of devoting herself to the Pillars of Islam as much as a man because of factors relating to her gender and role in society.

Consider the following verse, which condemns a woman's mind as deficient due to her lack of spiritual exercise:

> The women asked, "O Allah's Apostle! What is deficient in our intelligence and religion?" He said, "Is not the evidence of two women equal to the witness of one man?" They replied in the affirmative. He said, "This is the deficiency in her intelligence. Isn't it true that a woman can neither pray nor fast during her menses?" The women replied in the affirmative. He said, "This is the deficiency in her religion" (Bukhari 1.301).

The Islamic view of women in creation has brought the most dreadful results on Muslim wives, who, considered far less rational and far more emotional than men,[12] must be treated like children in need of direction. Male dominance is commanded in order to remove a woman's disobedience, including the administration of physical correction to help her moral and intellectual deficiencies (sura 4:34).

Ultimately, Islam teaches that woman was created for man. In one verse of the Qur'an, women are lumped together with other assets a man can acquire:

> Beautified for mankind is love of the joys (that come) from women and offspring; and stored-up heaps of gold and silver, and horses branded (with their mark), and cattle and land. That is comfort of the life of the world. Allah! With Him is a more excellent abode (sura 3:14 MGQ).

For Muslim women, this is what the Islamic world has to offer. This is why they were created.

Women and Spiritual Life

10

What is the spiritual influence of Muhammad's daughter Fatima?

The Prophet said, "Every year Gabriel used to revise the Qur'an with me once only, but this year he has done so twice. I think this portends my death, and you will be the first of my family to follow me." So I started weeping. Then he said. "Don't you like to be the mistress of all the ladies of Paradise or the mistress of all the lady believers?" So I laughed for that.

—Bukhari 4.819

Of Muhammad's four daughters, Fatima stands out to modern-day Muslims as the example to follow. In the well-known Hadith above, recollected by Fatima herself, Muhammad places his daughter at the fore of all Muslim women. Another tradition communicates the honor given her: "The most loved of women to the prophet is Fatima."[1] Islamic scholar John Esposito describes her as the embodiment of "dedication, suffering, and compassion," while Qur'anic scholar Yusuf Ali regards her as "one of the four perfect women."[2]

Given such praise and adulation, it is ironic that little is actually known about Fatima. Her childhood is undocumented. History is uncertain as to when she married the fourth leader of Islam, Ali. Little is recorded about her married life besides the birth of her two sons,

Husan and Husayn. She is not mentioned in the Qur'an outside of a passing reference to "ye Members of the Family" (sura 33:33). Early Islamic poetry, which honored the heroic age of the advent of Islam and its major characters, disregards her completely.

As Islamic critic Henri Lammens noted, "Fatima was reduced to being just a name, belonging to a real person, but remaining enigmatic—a ghost fading away before all efforts to get near her."[3] Her ultimate contribution can be summed up fairly easily: She was the daughter of Muhammad, the wife of Ali, and the mother of Husan and Husayn. Her spiritual duty was clear—please the men in her life and she would be pleasing to Allah.[4] Such is the greatest model Islam provides to women.

11

What is expected of women regarding the Pillars of Islam?

Every devout Muslim holds the Five Pillars of Islam as non-negotiable absolutes in life that must be followed without question or modification. To disregard any of them is to put one's eternal destiny in great jeopardy. They are as follows:

1. **The Creed** (*Shahada*): "There is no god but Allah. Muhammad is the messenger of Allah."

2. **Prayer** (*Salat*): Required five times daily, ritual prayer is the lifeline of the Muslim.

3. **Almsgiving** (*Zakat*): Each Muslim is obligated to give 2.5 percent of their income, after expenses, to the poor and needy.

4. **Fasting** (*Sawm*): Each adult Muslim must fast during the month of Ramadan. During this time, Muslims must, between sunrise and sunset, abstain from eating, drinking, sexual intercourse, and other worldly activities.

5. **Pilgrimage** (*Hajj*): The pilgrimage to Mecca is required of

all capable Muslims in order to honor Islam's establishment of monotheism through Abraham and Muhammad.[5]

The Five Pillars, foundational to the unity of the Islamic community, are extremely arduous and require a great deal from even the most devout followers of Muhammad. To fully dedicate oneself to these divinely prescribed tasks places perpetual strain on a person's time and energies, and is an impossibility for those who are physically deficient.

Additionally, certain periods of life, such as early motherhood, create more barriers to following the prophet's message. This did not go unnoticed by Muhammad, who had nearly a dozen wives, numerous concubines, and four daughters. He quickly recognized the need to adapt these religious duties to the female sex. Four of the five Pillars were amended, perhaps feminized, so that women too could follow them to the best of their abilities. After all, the hope of Paradise and the fear of hellfire were based on the command of strict adherence to these principles.

Prayer, the main Pillar in Islam, provides a clear picture regarding the differences between the sexes. Even though Muslims are quick to point out there is an equal obligation for prayer for all Muslims, Muhammad clearly delineated the restrictions and regulations in regard to women. First, men must be the leaders within the mosque, especially as it comes to the call to prayer (*adhan*), since women are not permitted to raise their voices in the mosque. Second, women are forbidden from leading the prayers if prayers are given in mixed company. Third, it is preferable that women pray at home, even though they are allowed to pray with men in congregational prayer.

> "The dog, the ass, and the woman interrupt prayer if they pass in front of the believer, interposing themselves between him and the *qiblah* (the direction of prayer)."

Congregational prayer, compulsory for all adult males, is optional (if put in the best light) for a woman. If women choose to come to congregational prayers, they are to pray in rows behind men.[6] The front rows are reserved for those of higher status, men. In fact, one Hadith comments as to why women are relegated to the back: "The dog, the ass, and the woman interrupt prayer if they pass in front of the believer, interposing themselves between him and the *qiblah* (the direction of prayer)."[7] Finally, if a mistake is made by the one leading in prayer (the *imam*), men will offer correction by stating, "*Subhanallah*" ("Exalted is Allah"), but women, expected to refrain from speaking, denote their disapproval by clapping. One Hadith declares, "Then Allah's Apostle said, 'Why did you clap so much? If something happens to anyone during his prayer he should say Subhan Allah. If he says so he will be attended to, for clapping is for women'" (Bukhari 1.652).

Thus, Muhammad discouraged women from practicing the very lifeline of Muslims—prayer—and at other times treated women's congregational prayers flippantly. Muhammad expressed far more interest in helping men prosper through prayer and worried that women could hinder that process (Bukhari 1.490). In fact, women have the ability to defile prayers, as the Qur'an itself remarks:

> O ye who believe! Draw not near unto prayer when ye are drunken, till ye know that which ye utter, nor when ye are polluted, save when journeying upon the road, till ye have bathed. And if ye be ill, or on a journey, or one of you cometh from the closet, or *ye have touched women,* and ye find not water, then go to high clean soil and rub your faces and your hands (therewith) (sura 4:43 MGQ, emphasis added).

The next two Pillars, almsgiving and fasting, basically require equal devotion from both sexes (sura 4:25; 57:18), although Muhammad, once again, recognizes the unique situation of women. In some cases, Muhammad wanted to ensure women were doing their part in building the Islamic community. One Hadith states,

> Once Allah's Apostle came out while Bilal was accompanying him. He went towards the women thinking that they had not heard him (that is, his sermon). So he preached to them and ordered them to pay alms. (Hearing that) the women started giving alms; some donated their earrings, some gave their rings and Bilal was collecting them in the corner of his garment (Bukhari 1.97).

However, in other cases, Muhammad interlinked fasting and

almsgiving for women who, for example, were physically incapable of holding the fast. He commanded, "For those who can do it (with hardship) is a ransom, the feeding of the one that is indigent" (2.184). Ibn Abbas said, "This Verse is not abrogated, but it is meant for old men and old women who have no strength to fast, so they should feed one poor person for each day of fasting (instead of fasting)" (Bukhari 6.32).

The final Pillar of Islam, and the climax of every Muslim's life, is the pilgrimage to Mecca, required of all Muslims who can afford the journey. This deed is especially important to women as this is their greatest accomplishment in working their way to Paradise. As noted in question 9, Muhammad encouraged women that "the best Jihad (for women) is Hajj Mabrur" (Bukhari 2.595).[9]

Muhammad would not obligate women in *jihad,* which he required of men: "Fighting is prescribed upon you, and ye dislike it" (sura 2:216). Ironically, in attempting to protect the Islamic community's mothers against the evils of war, Muhammad actually removed from them the only guaranteed promise of eternal life given in Islam, that of martyrdom (sura 3:190-195). Without the journey to Mecca, women have little hope of gaining entrance into heaven. And this chance diminishes even further when taking into consideration the final adage of Muhammad: "If a woman prays five [times a day], fasts Ramadan, *obeys her husband,* and guards her chastity, she will enter Heaven."[10]

Counting her obligation to her husband, it appears that a woman has *six* Pillars of Faith to fulfill.

12

How do women obtain eternal life in Islam?

As to the Righteous (they will be) in a position of Security, among Gardens and Springs; and We shall wed them to maidens with beautiful, big, and lustrous eyes.

—Sura 44:51-52,54

Islamic theology describes heaven in very masculine terms, as seen above. From a combination of Qur'anic texts, we can recognize at least four emphases of the Islamic Paradise:

- Using the imagery of "couches" or "thrones," Muslims are promised a "Home of Happiness and Dignity" (sura 56:15).

- Servants are promised to wait upon the righteous (sura 56:17).

- The righteous will fulfill every physical appetite with "the best of all foods," including wine (sura 83:23-26), water (sura 47:15), fowl (sura 56:21), and fruits (sura 38:51).

- Believers, specifically men, are given "chaste women" to fulfill every sexual desire (sura 38:52).[11]*

Muslim commentator Yusuf Ali, denigrating Muslim women in this life, described these perpetual virgins as "the society of Companions of the opposite sex, with beauty and charm but none of the grossness too often incidental to such companionship in this life."[12] Troublesome also is the fact that the man who enters eternal bliss is still married to his earthly wife. In addition, there is no guarantee that she will enjoy the same promises as her husband.[13]

If this portrait of heaven isn't demeaning and discouraging enough, Islamic theology in general provides even less solace to women who ponder the chances of eternity for their children. One Hadith in particular deals with a woman who had lost her infant in death and was looking to the prophet for comfort:

> A'isha, the mother of the believers, said that Allah's Messenger (may peace be upon him) was called to lead the funeral prayer of a child of the Ansar. I said: Allah's Messenger, there is happiness for this child who is a bird from the birds of Paradise for it committed no sin nor has he reached the age when one can commit sin. He said: A'isha, peradventure, it may be otherwise, because God created for Paradise those who are fit for it

---

* A man will "have the power of a hundred men"[14] to fulfill his desires with the most beautiful of women—which may perhaps include his wife.

> while they were yet in their father's loins and created for Hell
> those who are to go to Hell. He created them for Hell while
> they were yet in their father's loins (Muslim 33.6436).

Fatalism, deeply imbedded in the psyche of Islam, argues that Allah causes both good and evil; he causes some to go to heaven and others to go to hell. Here that fatalism rears its ugly head, dashing the hopes of a grieving mother that her innocent child would be in a better place. To the knowledgeable Muslim, heaven is promised in terms of family—there they will see "their fathers, their spouses and their offspring" (sura 13:23). Yet the picture can be quite gloomy for women, who, as we noted earlier, make up the majority of inhabitants in hell (Bukhari 1.28).

Therefore, women cling to the general promise that those who do more good deeds than bad will—if God wills (sura 14:4)—find themselves in heaven (sura 4:124). They hope in the tenuous promise that Allah will "remove their sins from them" (sura 48:5) and reunite them with their families (sura 40:8).

In contrast, the Bible offers hope to all women, both those who have sinned much and those who have sinned little. God promises to accept them and bring them to heaven if they place their trust in Jesus as the one who died for them.

Jesus said, "My Father's will is that everyone who looks to the Son and believes in him shall have eternal life, and I will raise him up at the last day" (John 6:40). The apostle Paul could say with full assurance that Jesus "saved us, not because of righteous things we had done, but because of his mercy" (Titus 3:5) and that "everyone who calls on the name of the Lord will be saved" (Romans 10:13).

Women and Family

13

What does Islam teach about the divinely ordained role of women in the family?

In both Christianity and Islam, the family is a divinely ordained institution in which society finds its basis. As such, the family unit is the cornerstone of civilization and the best barometer to measure the health of any culture. The Bible illustrates the preeminence of the family from its earliest words. After the creation account, God notes the joining of husband and wife, declaring that "a man shall leave his father and mother and be joined to his wife; and they shall become one flesh" (Genesis 2:24 NASB). The Qur'an in similar fashion declares,

> And among His Signs is this, that He created for you mates from among yourselves, that ye may dwell in tranquility with them, and He has put love and mercy between your (hearts): verily in that are Signs for those who reflect (sura 30:21).

Both sacred texts speak of the value of a wife (Proverbs 31; sura 3:14) and the blessing of children (Psalm 127:3; sura 42:49-51). Both command that children honor and obey their parents (Ephesians 6:1; sura 46:15). The family unit, argues each faith, should illustrate to an unbelieving world that God has displayed himself in power in the most intimate relationship a person will have in this life. Simply put, family should prove the trustworthiness of the faith.

What can quickly be seen, though, is that Christianity and Islam have widely different views on the subject of family. From polygamy to parenting, from chastity to childbearing, what can appear similar if viewed superficially is actually quite divergent if considered more critically. Islam is a repudiation of the Christian faith. Thus it rejects the biblical worldview of family in the same way it rejects the biblical view of God, revelation, salvation, and other crucial subjects. Just as Islamic texts revised the life of Christ, so too has Islam altered the family in order to fit its worldview and the life of its founder, Muhammad.

14

Why do Muslims arrange marriages?

In reaction to the emphasis on celibacy and the derogatory view of sex found within the Catholic Church of the early Middle Ages, Islam deemed marriage most appropriate for the propagation of the faith and the stability of society. Muslim scholars argue that Muhammad's piety is actually proven by his polygamy because it demonstrates his kindness in taking care of numerous women who needed his help.

> Male dominance is asserted, as it is usual for the woman to take the religion of her husband, and thereby his status is not affected.

Marriage itself is seen as "a religious duty and is consequently a moral safeguard as well as a social necessity."[1] Marriage's purpose and intent therefore cannot be fulfilled through any Western-style form of romance. Dating is forbidden in traditional Islam. A man and woman can get to know each other but are forbidden to be alone together. In fact, one tradition argues that if a Muslim man and woman are in a room alone, Satan is also present.

Certain principles apply when Muslims are considering their future partner and entering into a marriage contract:[2]

- Each party must consent to the proposed relationship. A woman's silence is recognized as consent according to Muhammad (Bukhari 9.79).

- The contract must be binding in perpetuity (with the exception of the temporary marriages found within Shi'a Islam).

- Two people must serve as witnesses to the marriage.

- The husband must provide a dowry (marriage gift) to the bride.

- The marriage must be public in its pronouncement.

- The woman must be free to marry. If she is widowed or divorced but expecting a child, she must wait until the child is born.

- The woman must be proven chaste, and not found to be involved in adultery or extramarital sex.

- The man and woman must have reached the age of puberty (seen in many Islamic countries as the age of nine for women).

- If the woman is a second, third, or fourth wife for the husband, the new bride must not be related to another wife.

Finally, the man is free to marry any monotheist, while the woman must marry a Muslim. The Qur'an stipulates, "(Lawful unto you in marriage) are (not only) chaste women who are believers, but chaste women among the People of the Book" (sura 5:5). Once again male dominance is asserted, as it is usual for the woman to take the religion of her husband, and thereby his status is not affected. Muhammad himself had one concubine who was a Christian (Maryam) and one who was a Jew (Rayhana).

15

Are Muslim wives treated as property?

Your wives are as a tilth [field] unto you; so
approach your tilth when or how ye will.

SURA 2:223

The imagery portrayed in the above verse is an unashamed picture of why, when, and how a Muslim husband is allowed to approach his wife as "ordained for [him] by Allah" (sura 2:222). One commentator proudly explained, "He sows the seed in order to reap the harvest. But he chooses his own time and mode of cultivation. He does not sow out of season nor cultivate in a manner which will injure or exhaust the soil. He is wise and considerate and does not run riot."[3]

Note, then, that the husband has absolute right over the woman sexually in timing, meaning, and method. He is the owner of the "field" and can subjectively decide when his wife should be "farmed." Beyond Allah's prohibitions, such as abstaining during menstruation (sura 2:222), he has ultimate power over her most intimate contacts.

A wife, according to Islamic teaching, will be chastised through angels for rejecting her suitor. One tradition relates, "If a husband calls his wife to his bed (that is, to have sexual relations) and she refuses and causes him to sleep in anger, the angels will curse her till morning" (Bukhari 4.460). This anger from Allah will carry forward until the husband is "pleased with her" (Muslim 2.3367).[4] For her disobedience, Allah will be deaf to a reluctant wife's prayers.[5] The seriousness of a wife's refusal is ultimately seen in the husband's ability to divorce his wife over her rejection (sura 66:5). As one Hadith concludes, "Wives are playthings, so take your pick."[6]

16

Is a Muslim woman's obedience to her husband incontestable?

Men are the protectors and maintainers of women, because Allah has given the one more (strength) than the other, and because they support them from their means. Therefore the righteous women are devoutly obedient, and guard in (the husband's) absence what Allah would have them guard. As to those women on whose part ye fear disloyalty and ill-conduct, admonish them (first), (next), refuse to share their beds, (and last) beat them (lightly).

—Sura 4:34

A Muslim woman's obedience to her husband is incontestable, according to the above verse, due to his physical superiority and financial provision. The husband does not simply praise his wife (or wives), he disciplines her whenever she is deemed ungrateful for his generosity, rebellious to his commands, or neglectful of his needs. His authority is in many ways unchallengeable, as one Hadith instructs, "A man will not be asked as to why he beat his wife" (Dawud 2142).

Muslim apologists reply swiftly that beatings are actually discouraged and that, although there is evidence that Muhammad refused to have sex with his wives during certain tense times, there is no evidence he ever beat any of his wives. Others assert that beating should only be as light as a feather and that it is intended as a symbol of humiliation, not as physical subjugation. Contemporary Islamic apologist Jamal Badawi affirmed that a beating may be appropriate as long as it is "a gentle pat to his wife that causes no physical harm to the body nor leaves any sort of mark."[7]

But although there is no evidence of Muhammad beating any of his wives or concubines, there is authenticated tradition that he cared very little about such beatings by other men and ignored abused women whom he considered unchaste or untrustworthy. The most striking example is found within the following Hadith:

> Rifa'a divorced his wife whereupon 'Abdur-Rahman bin Az-Zubair Al-Qurazi married her. 'Aisha said that the lady (came), wearing a green veil (and complained to her, 'Aisha) of her husband and *showed her a green spot on her skin caused by beating*)…'Aisha said, "I have not seen any woman suffering as much as the believing women. *Look! Her skin is greener than her clothes!*" When 'Abdur-Rahman heard that his wife had gone to the Prophet, he came with his two sons from another wife. She said, "By Allah! I have done no wrong to him but he is impotent and is as useless to me as this," holding and showing the fringe of her garment. 'Abdur-Rahman said, "By Allah, O Allah's Apostle! She has told a lie! I am very strong and can satisfy her but she is disobedient and wants to go back to Rifa'a." Allah's Apostle said, to her, "If that is your intention,

then know that it is unlawful for you to remarry Rifa'a *unless Abdur-Rahman has had sexual intercourse with you.*" Then the Prophet saw two boys with 'Abdur-Rahman and asked (him), "Are these your sons?" On that 'Abdur-Rahman said, "Yes." The Prophet said, "You claim what you claim (that is, that he is impotent) but by Allah, these boys resemble him as a crow resembles a crow" (Bukhari 7.715, emphasis added).

Here we find Muhammad as a marriage counselor, listening to the complaints of a couple with immense difficulties. The woman is severely battered and wishes to leave her husband. It seems she is even willing to lie in order to remove herself from the situation.

On the other hand, her husband comes prepared to illustrate that her accusations of impotency are patently false and therefore she cannot be trusted whatsoever. What is Muhammad's response to the woman found in this difficult situation? She must have sex with her abuser or she cannot divorce him and go back to her former husband! Secondly, there is deafening silence as to the marks on her body. Muhammad says not a word.[8]

17

Does Islam allow polygamy, concubines, and temporary marriages?

Ye are never able to do justice between wives even if it is your ardent desire: but turn not away (from a woman) altogether, so as to leave her (as it were) hanging (in the air).

—SURA 4:129

Islamic women face the fact that their monogamous relationship with their husbands can come to an end abruptly through any one of three options granted to their husbands. First, the Qur'an permits Muslim men to marry up to four women (sura 4:3) as long as each is treated equally monetarily and relationally. Second, the Qur'an allows Muslim conquerors to take concubines from among captives as long as they are not already married (sura 4:24). Finally, Shia Muslims, who number approximately 150 million today, allow temporary marriages (*mut'a*), marriages intended for a limited time only, which are intended to fulfill a man's sexual needs while traveling.

One tradition related that a temporary union "should last three nights, and if they like to continue, they can do so, and if they want to separate, they can do so."[9] Muhammad certainly allowed for these unions during wartime (Bukhari 6.139), but the vast majority of scholars contend that he revoked his proviso soon thereafter.[10]

18

Training children in the Islamic faith: What part does this play in the lives of Muslim women?

When she grows heavy, they both pray to Allah their Lord (saying): "If Thou givest us a goodly child, we vow we shall (ever) be grateful."

—SURA 7:189

The primary role of a Muslim woman, after pleasing her husband, is to bear children who will eventually grow up to be devout followers of Allah. So important are her duties that the upright mother is held up as the "best" companion of Muhammad (Bukhari 8.2). A child must obey the commands its mother transmits from her husband and must follow the mandate to not "be undutiful to one's parents" (Bukhari 8.7).

> Sisters will often submit to their brothers, seeing them as a type of man who is to come into their lives shortly.

In fact, to honor one's parents is listed alongside faithful prayers and participating "in Jihad in Allah's cause" (Bukhari 4.41). Fathers and mothers alike are commanded, "O ye who believe! Save yourselves and your families from a Fire whose fuel is Men" (sura 66:6). In Islamic sources, families are found both in Paradise (sura 13:23-24) and in hellfire (Bukhari 4.464).

A mother does not have much time to train her children properly. Unlike in non-Muslim cultures, where a young man or woman usually does not consider marriage until he or she is about 18, numerous Muslim countries arrange marriages by the time the children enter elementary school. Girls *as young as five* are already learning how to act like a wife and mother, how to be "docile, obedient, and self-sacrificing."[11] Males are regularly given priority in such basic settings as the family meal, where boys are given larger portions of food or women are allowed to eat only whatever is left over. As a result of this atmosphere, sisters will often submit to their brothers, seeing them as a type of man who is to come into their lives shortly.[12]

Most disturbing is the brutal ceremony of female circumcision, a rite millions of female infants have undergone, especially within the continent of Africa and the Middle East.[13] The custom is based on Muhammad's words about how a newborn is to be set aside for Allah: "I heard the Prophet saying, 'Five practices are characteristics of the [human nature]: circumcision, shaving the pubic hair, cutting the moustaches short, clipping the nails, and depilating the hair of the armpits'" (Bukhari 7.779). Though Islamic schools differ on the interpretation of this verse, circumcision was clearly established in early Islamic culture and was approved by Muhammad: "Circumcision is a law for men and a preservation of honour for women."[14] Today, the vast majority of Islamic scholars disagree only as to whether it is compulsory, recommended, or optional.[15]

Across North Africa, however, the practice is mandatory. It is maintained in this region that the practice does not involve mutilation but is a meticulous trimming of the infant's genital organ. In the tradition that specifies the procedure (Dawud 5251), the Arabic wording is ambiguous as to the extent of the cutting, but the more natural interpretation is that it involves the complete removal of the female organ of pleasure.

What is not ambiguous is the justification given by Muslim commentators. Health reasons are cited for male circumcision, but female circumcision, they say, "helps only to reduce the libido of the woman but does not do away with it, which is for the common good of society, and for her own good as well."[16] Another commentator puts it more bluntly: It will "tone down the sexual desire of the woman" and "diminish her lust."[17]

In a word, as with other Muslim beliefs and practices, female circumcision is performed to promote the well-being and pleasure of men and the subjugation of women.

19

What does Islam teach about divorce?

A divorce is only permissible twice; after that, the parties should either hold together on equitable terms, or separate with kindness.

—SURA 2:229

Muhammad knew the family must be the centerpiece of society and denounced divorce (*talaq*) as most "abominable" (Dawud 2172). His strong condemnation, though, does not make sense in light of the ease with which a man was allowed under Islamic law to divorce his wife or wives. The husband has rights over his wife (sura 2:228), while the woman is extremely limited in her rights to divorce. Unless she can prove impotence, insanity, or infidelity, the husband holds the ultimate power of divorce (Bukhari 7.213).

According to Islamic scholar John Esposito, divorce can be classified in five categories:[14]

1. *Divorce proper:* The husband has the right to divorce his wife by making a triple pronouncement of "I divorce you," which nullifies the marriage.

2. *Delegated divorce:* The husband delegates to his wife the power to divorce.

3. *Mutual divorce:* The husband grants the right to divorce upon request from his wife (sura 65:1) or by mutual acceptance of irreconcilable differences.

4. *Judicial process divorce:* While the husband has the unilateral right to divorce, a woman can bring to family court charges that may allow her to annul the marriage. Reasons include impotence or desertion.

5. *Apostasy divorce:* In one Islamic school, if the husband or wife leaves Islam, the marriage is automatically dissolved.

The Qur'an does guard wives in some ways. For example, a waiting period is required before a divorce is issued to ensure that the wife is not pregnant (sura 2:228*). Second, husbands can only divorce three times under Islamic law. Thereafter, the ex-wife can only come back to her first husband if she marries another man and consummates the union (sura 2:230). Third, the ex-husband is required to provide for the wife and children in a sufficient way (sura 2:233).

Nonetheless, it is apparent that a woman's rights in Islam are negligible at best. This is further illustrated by the fact that the husband is plainly delegated the custody of the children—girls when they are nine, and boys when they are seven. Even before these ages, he is required to supervise their handling while they are still in their mother's care during the early childhood years.[15] A wife and mother, supposedly highly honored in Islam, can lose the most important people in her life, and her husband is not even required to give a reason for his decision. She is simply abandoned.

---

* Sura 2:229 (see previous page) says "twice," but this is allowing for reconciliation. The third time is final, with the exception mentioned above.

20

What commands dominate the life of a devout Muslim woman?

*O ye who believe! Enter not the Prophet's houses, until leave is given
to you, for a meal (and then) not (so early as) to wait for its prepara-
tion: but when you are invited, enter; and when you have taken
your meal, disperse, without seeking familiar talk...And when
you ask (his ladies) for anything you want, ask them from before a
screen: that makes for greater purity for your hearts and for theirs.*

—Sura 33:53

Imagine that Muhammad invited a group of men to one of his
homes for a home-cooked meal. Imagine being the wife and hostess of
the event. Compare the scenario to one in your own home. The differences are significant. In the Islamic world, wives are simply asked
to demonstrate their purity by their absence. They are not to carry on
a long conversation with the opposite sex. Women are simply there to
serve without being noticed, without being heard.

As the Qur'an commands women, "Keep to accustomed speech.
Stay in your homes. Do not try to imitate the ostentatious clothes of
the women of the former times of ignorance. Get on with your prayers;
give alms and obey God and his Apostle" (sura 33:33).[16]

Keep...stay...get...give. These commands dominate the life of a
devout Muslim woman.

Women and Society

21

Humiliation or humility: Why are Muslim women required to wear a veil?

O Prophet! Tell thy wives and daughters, and the believing women, that they should cast their outer garments over their persons (when out of doors): that is most convenient, that they should be known (as such) and not molested. And Allah is Oft-Forgiving, Most Merciful.

—SURA 33:59

The veil (*hijab*), a word that literally means to conceal or to make invisible, is much debated and greatly misunderstood in the West. Millions of Muslim women around the world voluntarily wear traditional Islamic dress as a demonstration of humility, or out of a need to feel protected from worldly lusts. Many wear the *hijab* as a denunciation of Western morals, so easily seen in the lack of modest apparel among women, and to show pride in Islamic culture. Westerners must also realize that the mandate to cover is not simply a call to hide one's hair, but to conceal most of the body, excluding the hands and the face.

Many Islamic scholars, citing the Hadith (Bukhari 1.148), believe that all but the eyes must be covered. Furthermore, even that which is covered must also be acceptable according to Islamic law and custom. Muslim women are traditionally forbidden from wearing perfume or makeup, even if such things are concealed under modest garments.

Muhammad himself worried that perfume would cause the arousal of men, and he prohibited women wearing perfume from entering the mosque (Muslim 4.893). The woman who wore perfume in public, in mixed company, was a temptress, one who wished to seduce men into fornication (Dawud 7) or prostitution.

The veil (*hijab*) itself is quite cumbersome, as is noted by the policies which regulate its features:

- It must be thick, or else it is not considered acceptable, since it does not truly cover the woman's face. One Hadith affirms this, "Asma, the daughter of Abu Bakr entered upon the Messenger of God wearing a thin garment, and the Messenger of God turned away from her."

- It should not garner attention and should make the woman who wears it invisible (or at least unnoticeable).

- It must not be form-fitting, or else the woman is considered "dressed yet naked" and may be guilty of the attempted seduction of a man. Muhammad promised that these type of women "will not enter paradise."[1]

As sura 33:59 commands, a woman is required to place herself in full outward submission to Allah. If not, she runs the risk of being "molested." The idea of modesty—chastity—is thereby explicitly connected to a woman's clothing. If she is found without the covering, she has chosen to disobey Allah's instruction and therefore bears the brunt of responsibility for any consequences. The honor of her family is placed upon her shoulders.

As Geraldine Brooks eloquently explains, "The dangerous female body...has been made to carry the heavy burden of male honor."[2] Perhaps no one has better characterized the *hijab* than the American Samuel Zwemer (1867–1952), called "the Great Apostle to Islam," who wrote,

> In Arabia before the advent of Islam it was customary to bury female infants alive. Mohammed improved on the barbaric methods and discovered a way by which all females could be buried alive and yet live on—namely, the veil.[3]

22

How does Islam view women's education?

Thus have We sent this down—an Arabic Qur'an—and explained therein in detail some of the warnings, in order that they may fear Allah, or that it may cause their remembrance (of Him).

—SURA 20:113

It might be thought that Islam and education would go hand in hand because the Qur'an commands men and women to be knowledgeable of their religion's tenets. Islam's view of human beings would also seem to lend itself to the education of women, as Islamic theology declares mankind to be forgetful (sura 20:113) and weak (sura 4:28), and thus people must be guided properly (sura 4:175).

The Qur'an proclaims its own value in bringing wisdom: "This is the Book; in it is guidance sure, without doubt, to those who fear Allah" (sura 2:2). Allah himself is the source of all knowledge, commanding his disciples to "read!" (sura 96:1) and teaching "man that which he knew not" (sura 96:5).

The question must then be asked, Why among all religions of the earth do we find illiteracy so commonplace in countries where Islam predominates? For example, Pakistan's female literacy rate is 30 percent; Yemen's is 23.9 percent. At the same time, male literacy rates are significantly higher—58.9 percent in Pakistan and 66.6 percent in Yemen.[4] Further, the comparison of literacy by sex released by the United Nations in 2001 demonstrates that except for two countries (the United Arab Emirates and Qatar[5]) every Islamic nation had a male literacy rate higher (most of the time substantially higher) than the female rate.

> A woman is called to know about her religion, but her knowledge and participation is of secondary importance to that of the superior man.

These discrepancies, argue Muslim apologists, are not due to any

Islamic doctrine, but are to be blamed on the unfortunate circumstances "accelerated by catastrophic historical events such as the Mongol and Turkish invasions…[Women] were neglected and treated as sex objects, assumed heavy veiling, and were confined to their small circle of womenfolk with no contact outside their homes."[6] The Golden Age of Islam (AD 750–1250), an age where knowledge was treasured and the fields of medicine, philosophy, and the arts thrived in Islamic countries more than anywhere else in the civilized world, gave way to a new day that downgraded the position of women. More than seven centuries later, these invasions, along with Western colonialism, are blamed for the continued suppression of women's interests.

Muslim arguments aside, we have already seen that practices such as "heavy veiling" and women being treated as "sex objects" are founded in the Qur'an and were practiced by Muhammad himself. Even though there were times when women flourished under Islam, these were the exception to the norm and occurred in spite of Islamic principles.

Muhammad's third wife, Aisha, is a good illustration of a woman's role in Islam. Though certainly she was recognized as religiously credentialed because of her close proximity to Muhammad and her vast knowledge of his sayings,[7] overall her life is still an example of the Islamic diminishment of women. She transitioned from "playing in a swing with some of my girl friends" to being prepared for marriage: "Allah's Apostle came to me in the forenoon and my mother handed me over to him, and at that time I was a girl of nine years of age" (Bukhari 5.234).

As previously discussed, women are limited by the "deficiency of their minds" (Bukhari 3.826), they are encouraged to stay at home (sura 33:32-33), and they should basically expect whatever provisions they receive to come from their husbands' graciousness. Thus, a woman's education is integrally tied to how she is viewed as a person.

In essence, a woman is called to know about her religion, but her knowledge and participation is of secondary importance to that of the superior man. As we have seen, she is not required to participate in community prayers and not obligated to fight in holy war. She is considered a potential hindrance to prayers, especially if a man touches her before performing his prayers. She is excused from fasting due to her bodily cycles. In a word, the more she learns of her religion, the more she learns of the inferiority of her religious standing. Education has the great potential to discourage more education.

One Islamic reformist, Nimat Hafez Barazangi, considers this view of women, which so negatively affects education, and argues that human rights advocates must

> change misguided, misogynist interpretations, such as that men are in charge of women's moral and intellectual well-being (Sura 2:228, 4:34), and…modify the claim of the universality of human rights to include the specificity of self-realization.[8]

In a strong sense, Barazangi is absolutely correct. Until the words of Allah are changed or at least reinterpreted, it can only be expected that Islamic cultures that adhere strictly to the Qur'an will continue to discourage women and deprive them of many educational opportunities.

23

What is the Muslim perspective on women in the workplace?

And in no wise covet those things in which Allah hath bestowed His gifts more freely on some of you than on others: To men is allotted what they earn, and to women what they earn.

—SURA 4:32

Islamic law does not explicitly forbid women from working outside the home, a fact that is not surprising, since Muhammad's first wife, Khadijah, was herself a very successful merchant and trader. Her ability to accumulate wealth was a great asset to her husband in the formation of Islam. However, according to traditional Islam, there are certain rules that must be followed in order for women to be allowed to work outside the home:[9]

- A woman cannot neglect her duties as wife and mother.
- A woman cannot work alongside men where there is potential for physical interaction.
- A woman should work at a place suited to her physical and mental capacities (Bukhari 7.773).

As can be seen, several problems arise from the above stipulations. A woman's first obligation, as mother and wife, is controlled by her husband. His acceptance of her added responsibilities is not very likely for numerous reasons, not the least of which is that he, as husband, is responsible for the financial obligations of the house. If his wife is working outside the home, a husband could see her work as an admission that he is unable to provide for the family.

Second, many Muslims struggle with the prohibition against women's working alongside men other than their husbands. A woman is to be guarded carefully and not placed in risky situations. This regulation is especially difficult to follow in the West, but many anti-Western Islamic scholars point to the grave immorality seen in the workplace in Western countries as an added rationale for this ban.

Further, Islamic scholars demand that a woman's modesty be guarded from the unfettered freedoms of the West. At the very least, a woman cannot work in a situation where she could be left alone with a man not her husband, or placed in a situation where her character could be put in question. She is to be removed from any situation in which men are challenging her chastity (Bukhari 4.28).

Finally, there is the issue of a woman being accompanied by a male authority known as a *mahram*. This person—most likely her husband, father, or brother—escorts the woman from place to place and safeguards her chastity. Thus, even though many women worked alongside Muhammad, they did not work outside his authority. That is, they may have worked in aiding the prophet, but he was always present on those occasions. He accompanied them, thereby guarding their virtue.

However, the situation of today's working Islamic woman is not even remotely similar and cannot be reasonably compared to the example of Muhammad's women. Women stepping out into the workplace today run the danger of disobeying the restraints of the Qur'an,[10] which declares,

> It is no sin for them (thy wives) to converse freely with their fathers, or their sons, or their brothers, or their brothers' sons, or the sons of their sisters or of their own women, or their slaves. O women! Keep your duty to Allah. Lo! Allah is ever Witness over all things (sura 33:55 MGQ).

24

Why does Islam exclude women from politics?

I found (there) a woman ruling over them and provided with every requisite; and she has a magnificent throne. I found her and her people worshipping the sun besides Allah.

—SURA 27:23-24

At first glance, it could be assumed that the verse cited above is promoting the leadership of a woman, the Queen of Sheba. Here, a nation benefits from the wise and prudent leadership of the queen, who heeds the advice of King Solomon and submits to Islam (according to sura 27:44). However, the passage has little to do with female leadership and more to do with encouraging all nations to join in the praise of Allah. Furthermore, the Queen of Sheba's leadership preceded the advent of Islam and fell in what Muslim scholars call the Time of Ignorance.

Upon Muhammad's arrival, a new age arose, an epoch in which the House of Islam, led by a successor of Muhammad (a *caliph*) would rightly guide the Muslim community. Moreover, Muhammad, in the only Hadith dealing explicitly with the subject of female political leaders, vehemently argued against such a notion, declaring that, "such people as ruled by a lady will never be successful" (Bukhari 5.709). Yet the landscape of Islamic history is sprinkled with female leaders such as Queen Orpha of Yemen (died AD 1090) and Sultana Radia of Delhi (thirteenth century).[11] But it is more noteworthy that, as one author pointed out, "In Arabic-speaking countries no woman has yet been a leader of the state."[12]

Although the above tradition excludes women from the head of state, Muslims recognize that it does not explicitly bar them from lower levels of leadership. Some Muslim scholars even argue that women *must* be involved in politics because they are an integral part of the community (*umma*) of Islam. And while most Islamic scholars reject women as judges, some now argue that there are no prohibitions in the Qur'an or Hadith against female judges.[13] Yet the traditional argument would not allow female judges, because they would be making religious decisions over men, something anathematized until recently. As a whole, it is evident that Islam does little to encourage female political leadership and scarcely even discusses the subject.

Above all else, women are to be wives and mothers. The entire system of Islam, itself innately political, depends on women raising up generations of Muslims who will strictly adhere to Islamic beliefs and practices. Without their contribution, the House of Islam would crumble. How ironic it is that the house that they uplift denigrates their value in so many ways.

Women and Infidelity

25

Sexual infidelity: What does Islam teach?

As for those of your women who are guilty of lewdness, call to witness four of you against them. And if they testify (to the truth of the allegation) then confine them to the houses until death take them or (until) Allah appoint for them a way (through new legislation).

—Sura 4:15 MGQ

The Qur'an seems to indicate that those found in adultery be given 100 lashes (Sura 24:2), a very severe punishment. However, the Hadith is quite explicit in pronouncing the death sentence by stoning for those found to be unfaithful to their spouse (Bukhari 2.413; Muslim 4211). Why the discrepancy?

Muslim scholars, although not unanimous, draw a distinction between premarital sex (fornication) and marital infidelity (adultery), even though the Arabic term for both acts is the same

> "The passage on stoning, we read it, we were taught it, and we heeded it. The apostle stoned and we stoned them after him."

(*zina*). *Fornication* is sex between a man and a woman, neither of which are married. *Adultery* is sex between a man and a women with one or both under marriage contract. In the latter case, both are guilty of adultery.

Because of Islam's strong emphasis on women's chastity, family unity, and community purity, adultery is taken very seriously within

Islamic society. Therefore, early Islamic sources clearly affirm stoning as rightful punishment for the vile act. Consider the following:

- The earliest biography of Muhammad, written by Ibn Ishaq (died AD 767), confirms that Muhammad taught and practiced stoning. Umar, the second leader of Islam, testified, "Part of what he sent down was the passage on stoning, we read it, we were taught it, and we heeded it. The apostle stoned and we stoned them after him."

- Different scholars who have authenticated Muhammad's words universally substantiate Muhammad's approval of stoning.[1]

- Modern commentators also confirm stoning. Yusuf Ali writes, "Although *zina* covers both fornication and adultery, in the opinion of Muslim jurists, the punishment laid down here applies only to unmarried persons. As for married persons, their punishment, according to the *Sunna* [example] of the Prophet (peace be on him), is stoning to death."[2]

A few situations allow for a more lenient penalty, such as a reasonable certification that an adulterer is insane (Dawud 4388). On the other hand, there are numerous ways to prove guilt. Most explicitly, sura 24:4 declares that the one who accuses a person of adultery (or fornication) may prove it by producing four witnesses. Self-incrimination, either by confession or through obvious evidence such as pregnancy, is another route of proving guilt. One Hadith (Bukhari 8.814, see the next question) recounts an occasion on which Muhammad was confronted by an adulterer who repeated his confession four times. Muhammad "ordered him to be stoned to death" (Dawud 4364).

Some safeguards exist. If someone is convicted of falsely accusing a chaste woman, a penalty of 80 lashes is prescribed. The slanderer's right to civic responsibility is abrogated unless they "repent thereafter and mend (their conduct)" (sura 24:5).

In a final point of irony, however, this safeguard demonstrates how the judicial system of Islam breaks down when cases of rape are involved. When a woman accuses a man of raping her, she is required by law to prove the man's guilt or, according to the Qur'an, she herself will be found guilty of lying about the man's character (sura 24:4-7). The consequences that follow in Islamic countries, even including such semi-secular nations as Pakistan and Nigeria, are extreme. First, the woman could be punished with the above-mentioned 80 lashes. However, the more horrifying result is that she has now proclaimed her own infidelity, thus incriminating herself and possibly facing death by stoning.

26

What is a modern-day example of an execution to purify the Muslim community? (The story of Soraya M.)

A man from among the people, came to Allah's Apostle while Allah's Apostle was sitting in the mosque, and addressed him, saying, "O Allah's Apostle! I have committed an illegal sexual intercourse." The Prophet turned his face away from him. The man came to that side to which the Prophet had turned his face, and said, "O Allah's Apostle! I have committed an illegal intercourse." The Prophet turned his face to the other side, and the man came to that side, and when he confessed four times, the Prophet called him and said, "Are you mad?" He said, "No, O Allah's Apostle!" The Prophet said, "Are you married?" He said, "Yes, O Allah's Apostle." The Prophet said (to the people), "Take him away and stone him to death."

—BUKHARI 8.814

The example that Muhammad set nearly 1400 years ago found its way into the small village of Kupayeh in southwestern Iran. There, a married woman and mother of nine children by the name of Soraya (born in 1951) had been found guilty of adultery and was waiting for her death sentence to be carried out.

Finally, the day arrived and Soraya was escorted to the town square. Her body, cloaked in a simple white dress, was carefully placed into a hole especially dug for this occasion. Only her head and shoulders were exposed. A large crowd had gathered, and they were anticipating the mayor's orders to execute the sentence. The mayor motioned the crowd to step back at least 20 feet, and he used Soraya's head as the center of a precise circle he marked out. Then he grabbed a stone and handed it to Soraya's father: "It is to you that befalls the honor of throwing the first stone...Please proceed."[3]

Her father exclaimed, "Allah be Praised!" and threw the stone, although missing the target. He missed numerous times and finally gave the right to Ghorban-Ali, Soraya's husband. The mayor encouraged the husband, stating, "May God guide your arm." After a few throws one stone hit the mark, hitting his wife on the forehead. Next, two of their sons simultaneously threw stones, one of which struck her on the head and caused her head to jerk back violently. Finally, it was Sheikh Hassan's turn. As he held his Qur'an in his left hand, he excited the crowd by proclaiming, "I am not the one who is throwing the stone... It is God who is guiding my arm...It is he who commands me and the revenge I am meting out is not for me."

The agonizing brutality finally ended as Soraya breathed her last. At that moment the crowd, in near riot, rejoiced, "God is great...Praise be to God." As quickly as the stoning began, it was over. The crowd dispersed and returned to their daily lives. Soraya's body was left for the dogs until a few women in the village covered her with a simple sheet. As for Soraya, the only remaining memory of her is one sole photograph, taken by an itinerant photographer when she was just nine years old.[4]

27

Spiritual infidelity: How does Islam respond to women who turn from Allah?

Some Zanadiqa (atheists) were brought to 'Ali and he burnt them. The news of this event, reached Ibn 'Abbas who said "If I had been in his place, I would not have burnt them, as Allah's Apostle forbade it, saying, 'Do not punish anybody with Allah's punishment (fire).' I would have killed them according to the statement of Allah's Apostle, 'Whoever changed his Islamic religion, then kill him.'"

—BUKHARI 9.57

The highest treason against Allah is not adultery but apostasy. The general principle is found within the first chapters of the Qur'an: "If anyone desires a religion other than Islam (submission to Allah) never will it be accepted of him" (sura 3:85). Immediate retribution was clearly the practice of Muhammad's contemporaries. This was the case with a Jewish man, as told in a Hadith. An accusation is brought:

> "He was a Jew and became a Muslim and then reverted back to Judaism." Then Abu Muisa requested Mu'adh to sit down but Mu'adh said, "I will not sit down till he has been killed. This is the judgment of Allah and His Apostle ["] (for such cases) and repeated it thrice. Then Abu Musa ordered that the man be killed, and he was killed (Bukhari 9.58).

Some Muslim apologists vehemently argue that Islam is not a violent religion and repeatedly quote the phrase, "Let there be no compulsion in religion" (sura 2:256). A number of Islamic countries have even signed documents that support religious freedom, such as the United Nations' Covenant on Civil and Political Rights—nations including Afghanistan, Egypt, Iran, Libya, and Sudan. The covenant demands freedom of religion for all citizens.[5]

But any casual observer of Islamic states knows full well that none of these countries practice freedom of religion. The Islamic government in Sudan has, through its holy warriors, killed more than 1.5 million Christians, mostly in the south of the country. Afghanistan, even after its liberation from the Taliban, still practices execution of infidels, as was seen in 2006 with a convert by the name of Rahman. Although the Muslim-turned-Christian's life was eventually spared due to international outcry, the situation exposed Afghanistan's Islam-based constitution, which mandates that infidels must be put to death.[6]

Simply stated, to most Muslim scholars religious freedom means a person *born* a Jew or a Christian has the right to remain in his religion as long as he follows certain rules put in place centuries ago.[7] But a person born Muslim is not afforded the same right to convert to any other religion, since he or she has seen the superior truth of Islam and thus cannot legitimately turn his back on Allah. Of course, it is perfectly fine for a Christian or a Jew to become a Muslim at any time, and no one can forbid the conversion.

Disagreements arise as to how to handle female infidels. It seems clear from numerous passages of the Qur'an that women are not excluded from the death penalty—for example, sura 4:90-91. One Muslim commentator wrote of this passage, "Whosoever turns back from his belief (*irtada*), openly or secretly, take him and kill him wheresoever ye find him, like any other infidel."[8] Muslims, according to one tradition, are even rewarded "on the day of resurrection" if they kill infidels[9] (though a small minority of Muslim jurists argues for greater leniency for female apostates).

Here is a brief synopsis of what could happen to a woman who rejects her Islamic faith:

- She is to be imprisoned until such time as she recants her new faith and reverts to Islam. It is allotted that she can be whipped up to 39 times daily.

- If she and her husband become Christians in a territory that is subsequently taken over by Islam, she (along with her children) can be made a slave.

- If all else fails, she must be forced to revert to Islam if she does not "willingly" submit.

- If she dies, her property is to be distributed to her Muslim family or to the government.[10]

If an apostate woman survives such brutality, her husband will almost certainly divorce her and receive full custody of the children. She will be ostracized by her family and by society. It will become nearly impossible for her to gain employment, and she will be left isolated, with no money and little earthly hope.

Women and Jesus

28

Biblical fidelity: Why do Muslim women risk everything to become Christians?

Why have so many women chosen the narrow and painful road to Christ? What reasons do they give as to why they surrender everything—literally—and follow the Lord Jesus?

One Iranian woman, Sharareh, spoke of the tremendous grace found within Christianity and the overwhelming emptiness found within Islam. She made the pilgrimage to Mecca but "didn't feel anything when I went there and came back."

However, upon hearing a Christian pastor, she said, "He was speaking on the topic of God taking your burdens for you, and I realized God was calling me, and I felt at peace being there."[1] What a contrast to the Qur'an, which declares, "If one heavily laden should call another to (bear) his load, not the least portion of it can be carried (by the other)" (sura 35:18).

> Today, there are more than 700 million Muslim women who live under the bondage of Islam.

A young Saudi woman, Aisha, struggled with surrendering her life to Jesus Christ because she would have to admit that her devout Muslim father, who had recently died, was separated from God for all eternity. She knew in her mind that Christ was Savior, but her heart hesitated to accept the truth. She challenged God to prove himself real to her. She recalled,

> I told Jesus that I would believe in Him if He would prove that He was God…Jesus…appeared to me in a dream. He told me that He loved my father, but my father refused to believe in Him. I never knew that my father had a chance to know Jesus, but Jesus said he did have a chance. "It is too late for your father, but it is not too late for you. I love you too," Jesus told me. He loves me! I asked [a Christian friend] to tell me one more time how he had met Jesus and found peace. As I listened…I bowed my head at that table and prayed to receive Jesus Christ as my Lord and Savior.[2]

Tatiana, a young woman from Kyrgyzstan, described how the Scripture's life-changing power had made the eternal difference in her life. She explained,

> I steadily gained a passion for reading the Bible. I even began going to the Bible readings when Peter himself [a friend] did not attend. After reading the New Testament, I was convinced that Jesus Christ truly is the Son of the living God. One night at the Bible reading I confessed Jesus as my personal Lord and Savior.[3]

Undeserved grace. Unconditional love. Incontrovertible truth. These are the attributes Christians must always keep in mind when sharing Christ with a Muslim woman (or with anyone, for that matter). It is still an amazing experience to realize the power of the gospel to change someone's life. And it is heartbreaking to recognize the power of false religion to destroy someone's life.

Today, there are more than 700 million Muslim women who live under the bondage of Islam. Our prayer is that they be set free.

May they "know Him and the power of His resurrection and the fellowship of His sufferings, being conformed to His death" (Philippians 3:10 NASB). Truth is Immortal.

29

What does Jesus offer to Muslims who desire eternal life?

If you are a Muslim who wants to know that God has accepted you, forgiven you, and has given you eternal life, what can you do? Jesus promises that everyone who believes on him can know that they *now* possess eternal life:

- "I tell you the truth, whoever hears my word and believes him who sent me *has eternal life* and will not be condemned; he has *crossed over* from death to life" (John 5:24).

- "I tell you the truth, he who believes has eternal life" (John 6:47).

Specifically, what does God want us to believe and trust in so we can have eternal life with him?

First, we must realize we have broken God's laws—if we were to die today, we would stand guilty before God and be eternally condemned. God bluntly states, "The soul who sins is the one who will die" (Ezekiel 18:4).

How can we know what sin is and if we have committed it? The Bible tells us that "through the Law comes the knowledge of sin" (Romans 3:20 NASB). The law would include the Ten Commandments and Jesus' Sermon on the Mount. A clear way to discover if we have broken God's law is found in Matthew 22. Jesus was asked,

> "Teacher, which is the greatest commandment in the law?" Jesus replied, "Love the Lord your God with all your heart and with all your soul and with all your mind. This is the first and greatest commandment. And the second is like it: 'Love your neighbor as yourself.' All the law and the prophets hang on these two commandments" (verses 36-40).

Can any of us say we have loved God with all our heart, all our mind, and all our soul every moment we have lived? Would any of us tell God we had always loved our neighbor as we love ourselves? If we can't say yes to these two commands, then according to Jesus we are guilty of breaking the two greatest commandments God has given. We have sinned greatly! Further, we all know we are guilty of having committed other sins. The Bible says, "We know that whatever the law says, it says…so that every mouth may be silenced and the whole world held accountable to God" (Romans 3:19).

To address this problem of lawbreaking and sin, Islam and all religions besides Christianity teach we must do certain things and keep certain laws, such as the Five Pillars of Islam. We are told to do this so we may perhaps merit God telling us, "You have done enough. I will give you Paradise because of what you have done." In Islam, for instance, a person must outweigh his or her bad works by accumulating good works, hoping to achieve at least half good works. But even then, Islam teaches that Allah's mercy is not assured.

Second, Christianity is the only religion in the world that teaches that no man or woman can satisfy the requirements of God by what we might do. Rather, the Bible teaches that God himself made the way for us to be forgiven. God sent his Son, Jesus, into the world to live a sinless, perfect life in order to provide for us the perfect righteousness we need to stand before God. Further, Jesus willingly died on the cross, where the sins of the world were placed on him. He experienced the full punishment of God that we deserve. In other words, he became our sin-bearer so that we need not be punished. God sent him to pay for our sins. This sounds too good to be true, but this is the good news of the gospel.

Where does the Bible teach that God sent Christ to pay the penalty for all our sins? The apostle Peter wrote, "Christ died for sins once for all, the righteous for the unrighteous, to bring you to God" (1 Peter 3:18). Jesus didn't have any sins of his own. He voluntarily became our substitute and died in our place. Everything that needed to be done to satisfy God's justice and holiness regarding our sin, Christ did for us while on the cross.

Jesus paid a debt we could never pay. Why? Because we committed our sins against an infinite, loving God, acts which deserve an infinite punishment. We couldn't pay an infinite punishment, but Jesus could. Jesus is the Son of God. Luke records this fact when describing one of Jesus' trials. "They all said, 'Are you the Son of God, then?' And he said to them, 'Yes, I am'" (Luke 22:70 NASB). As the Son of God, Jesus brought the good news that "God did not send his Son into the world to condemn the world, but to save the world through him" (John 3:17).

Where does the Bible teach that God credits the righteousness of Christ's perfectly lived life to our account so we can stand unblemished before God? Paul writes,

> To the man who does not work [that is, one who does not do good works to earn God's favor] but trusts God who justifies the wicked, his faith is credited as righteousness (Romans 4:5).

God credits to you the righteousness of Christ's sinless life the moment you place your faith in Christ. "This righteousness from God comes through faith in Jesus Christ to all who believe" (Romans 3:22).

Third, believing on Jesus is not just accepting facts about him. True belief is when you transfer all of your trust to Jesus to save you. When you do, you can know for certain you will go to heaven. Why? Because the gift of salvation depends on Jesus living the perfect life, not you. Jesus already lived his perfect life and is now in heaven. The basis of our salvation is eternally secure.

We must realize we are all sinners and believe Jesus is the Son of God, that he lived a sinless life, that he died on the cross as a substitute for our sins, and then rose from the dead.

What does it mean to transfer all of our trust to Jesus and to believe in him to save us? Do you recall hearing a story about a man who walked across Niagara Falls on a tightrope? The crowd on the banks of the river was amazed. The man then proceeded to place 200 pounds of sandbags in a wheelbarrow and pushed the wheelbarrow across the falls. After doing this a few times, he finally spoke to the crowd and asked, "How many of you believe I can take this wheelbarrow across

> "God did not send his Son into the world to condemn the world, but to save the world through him. Whoever believes in him is not condemned."

the falls again—with a person inside?" They all shouted they believed he could. Then he asked, "Which one of you will be the first to get in?"

Their belief he could do that was an intellectual faith, but trust would require them to get into the wheelbarrow. It's one thing to say you believe in Christ; it's another to entrust yourself into his hands. Would you be willing to right now put yourself into Christ's hands and ask him to forgive your sins and be your Savior and Lord? If you sincerely want to trust Jesus right now, you can do so by praying the following prayer to receive Jesus Christ as your personal Lord and Savior:

> *Dear Jesus,*
>
> *I acknowledge my sinfulness before you. I confess that I have been trying to earn my own salvation by following the teachings of the Qur'an. But I now realize that Allah is not the true God. I recognize my need for forgiveness and I understand that Christ died for my sins on the cross so I wouldn't have to be punished. I now trust in and receive you as my personal Savior and Lord. Come into my life, live in me, and give me courage and strength to face the opposition I may encounter. From this moment on, I will trust that you will take me to heaven when I die, as you promised. In Jesus' name I pray. Amen.*

Remember the promise of eternal life to those who believe:

> God so loved the world that he gave his one and only Son, that whoever believes in him shall not perish but have eternal life. For God did not send his Son into the world to condemn the world, but to save the world through him. Whoever believes in him is not condemned, but whoever does not believe stands condemned already because he has not believed in the name of God's one and only Son (John 3:16-18).

I write these things to you who believe in the name of the

Son of God so that you may know that you have eternal life
(1 John 5:13).

If you have prayed to receive Christ, please write us at *The John Ankerberg Show* or e-mail us at thetruth@johnankerberg.org so we can send you some helpful materials about growing in the Christian life. We also recommend that you begin to read the New Testament to know more about the true Jesus Christ. In addition, attend a church that honors Christ as Lord and teaches the Bible as God's Word. Talk to God daily in prayer.

For additional spiritual growth resources,
please visit our Web site at www.johnankerberg.org.

For more information about the ministry of Emir Caner,
please visit www.emircaner.com.

Additional Resources
on Islam and Women

Additional important materials are available from the following organizations:

www.AlwaysBeReady.com: The Web site of speaker and author Charlie Campbell, which includes several Muslim articles and media resources.

www.Answering-Islam.org: Provides an in-depth historical and biblical response to doctrines of Islam and counters claims of Islamists. Includes an encyclopedia of Islam.

www.ApologeticsIndex.org: A huge directory of free apologetics resources featuring a quality overview of Islam with documented links.

www.BeThinking.org: Apologetics resources for free, with several specific to Islam, from a European Evangelical perspective.

www.CARM.org: The Christian Apologetics Resource Ministry (CARM) with a selection of short-answer articles on aspects of Islam as it relates to Christianity.

www.EmirCaner.com: A former Muslim turned Christian professor who is now president of Truett-McConnell College.

www.ErgunCaner.com: A former Muslim who is now a Christian and president of Liberty Baptist Theological Seminary.

www.ImpactApologetics.com: An online store representing a wide selection of apologetics-specific materials, including several audio downloads.

www.LeaderU.edu: This Campus Crusade for Christ resource offers an extensive array of academic articles on world religions, including many on Islam.

www.LeeStrobel.com: This Web site offers short video clips of leading scholars debating issues of Islam from a Christian perspective.

Notes

Why the Truth Matters
Section One: Influential Women in the Life of Muhammad

1. Ergun Mehmet Caner, ed., *Voices Behind the Veil* (Grand Rapids, MI: Kregel Publications, 2003), 63. Upon becoming pregnant, expectant mothers often recite sura 1 (*Al-Fatiha,* "The Opening") and sura 36 (*Ya-Sin,* the name of the two Arabic letters that begin it). See also Norma Tarazi, *The Child in Islam* (Plainfield, IN: American Trust Publications, 1995).

2. "The Prophet (peace be upon him) said: A boy is in pledge for his Aqiqah, Sacrifice is made for him on the seventh day, his head is shaved and he is given a name" (Dawud 2832). See also www .aqiqahkorban.com/aqiqah.html.

3. "The Prophet (peace be upon him) said: On the Day of Resurrection you will be called by your names and by your fathers' names, so give yourselves good names" (Dawud 4930).

4. "A son was born to me and I took him to the Prophet, who named him Ibrahim, did *tahneek* for him with a date, invoked Allah to bless him and returned him to me" (Sahih Bukhari 7.376). In another Hadith, Muhammad performs the ritual and then names the baby Abdullah.

5. Sura 33:21, "Ye have indeed in the Messenger of Allah an excellent exemplar for him who hopes in Allah and the Final Day, and who remember Allah much."

6. The Five Pillars include the creed (*shahada*), prayers (*salat*), almsgiving (*zakat*), fasting (*sawm*), and the pilgrimage (*hajj*). The six fundamental beliefs include belief in one god (*tawhid*), angels, revelation, prophets, judgment, heaven, and hell. See Ergun Caner and Emir Caner, *Unveiling Islam* (Grand Rapids, MI: Kregel Publications, 2002), 121-31, 145.

7. Muslims will disagree with this statement and argue that the first Muslim woman was Eve. Obviously, the authors believe that the first Muslim woman was Khadijah, the first wife of Muhammad, who accepted the Islamic faith almost immediately upon his first revelation.

8. Haifaa A. Jawad, *The Rights of Women in Islam* (New York: St. Martin's Press, 1998), 1.

9. Said Abdullah Seif al-Hatimy, *Woman in Islam: A Comparative Study* (Lahore, Pakistan: Islamic Publications, 1979), 17-8.

10. See also sura 81:8-14, in which the Qur'an declares that on Judgment Day, the innocent victim of infanticide will find justice as the "scrolls are laid open" (v. 10) and the "Blazing Fire is kindled to fierce heat" (v. 11).

11. Ibn Warraq, *Why I Am Not a Muslim* (New York: Prometheus Books, 1995), 292. Warraq quotes Ahmed al-Ali, *Organisations Sociales chez les Bedouins,* as evidencing the rarity of female infanticide.

12. Warraq, 292.

13. Warraq, 292-3. Women also served as judges, estate owners, and traders.

14. Ibn Ishaq, *The Life of Muhammad,* tr. Alfred Guillaume (London: Oxford University Press, 1955), 71.

15. Ishaq, 71.

16. Muhammad Haykal, *The Life of Muhammad,* tr. Isma'il al Faruqi (Plainfield, IN: American Trust Publications, 1976), 53.

17. Henri Lammens, "The Koran and Tradition: How the Life of Muhammad was Composed," in Ibn Warraq, ed., *The Quest for the Historical Muhammad* (New York: Prometheus Books, 2000), 173.

18. *The Holy Qur'an: English Translation of the Meanings and Commentary* (Al-Medinah, Saudi Arabia: King Fahd Holy Qur'an Printing Complex, AH 1410), 1971, fn 6184.

19. Haykal, 62.

20. William Muir, *Mahomet and Islam* (New York: Fleming H. Revell Company, n.d.), 20.

21. Phil Parshall, *Lifting the Veil: The World of Muslim Women* (Waynesboro, GA: Gabriel Publishing, 2002), 26.

22. See Parshall, 26-7. He notes, "In almost all Islamic countries, it is strictly forbidden for men and women to touch in public, even if married to each other...So much for following the example of the Prophet!"

23. See Karen Armstrong, *Muhammad* (San Francisco: Harper San Francisco, 1992), 158.

24. Maulana Muhammad Ali, *Living Thoughts of the Prophet Muhammad* (Columbus, OH: Ahmadiyya Society for the Propagation of Islam, 1992), 30. See also the short article by the same organization at www.muslim.org/islam/aisha-age.htm#_ftn4.

25. Al-Hatimy, 105. He writes, "We should remember that this took place 1,400 years ago and at the desert of Arabia, where girls mature at an early age."

26. "Eight-Year-Old Girl Divorces Husband from Arranged Marriage," April 16, 2008, www.foxnews .com/story/0,2933,351388,00.html.

27. Warraq, 99.

28. Ergun Caner and Emir Caner, *Unveiling Islam,* 59.

29. Warraq, 101.

Section Two: Women in the Creation Order

1. Haifaa A. Jawad, *The Rights of Women in Islam* (New York: St. Martin's Press, 1998), 6.

2. For further study on Islam and fatalism, see Ergun Caner and Emir Caner, *Unveiling Islam* (Grand Rapids, MI: Kregel Publications, 2002), 241-42.

3. Millard Erickson, *Christian Theology* (Grand Rapids, MI: Baker Book House, 1983), 515.

4. Michael Novak, "Another Islam," *First Things* (November 2002), accessed at www.firstthings.com/article.php3?id_article=2090.

5. Novak.

6. See also sura 48:5 and 57:12.

7. As will be seen later, women are removed from responsibilities due to physiological reasons. A woman does not have to pray when menstruating and is not called to *jihad* (holy war).

8. Also repeated in Bukhari 4.611.

9. Repeated in 7.114.

10. Said Abdullah Seif al-Hatimy, *Women in Islam: A Comparative Study* (Lehore, Pakistan: Islamic Publications, 1979), 21-2.

11. This is not to say women did not fight in war. Aisha, the young wife of Muhammad, even fought in war against other Muslims and was defeated at the Battle of the Camel.

12. Al-Hatimy, 37-8.

Section Three: Women and Spiritual Life

1. Quoted in Andrew Rippin, *Muslims: Their Religious Beliefs and Practices,* 2nd ed. (New York: Routledge, 2001), 114.

2. Ergun Mehmet Caner, ed. *Voices Behind the Veil* (Grand Rapids, MI: Kregel Publications, 2003), 49.

3. Henri Lammens, "Fatima and the Daughters of Muhammad," in Ibn Warraq, ed., *The Quest for the Historical Muhammad* (Amherst, NY: Prometheus Books, 2000), 279.

4. For further explanation, see Ibn Warraq, *Why I Am Not a Muslim* (New York: Prometheus Books, 1995), 313. Warraq speaks of one Hadith in which Muhammad demands Fatima stay at home and fulfill her chores.

5. See Samuel Zwemer, *Islam* (New York: Student Volunteer Movement for Foreign Missions, 1907), 102-13.

6. Sheikh M.S. al-Munajjid, "Differences in Prayer for Men and Women," at www.islamqa.com/index.php?ref=1106&ln=eng.

7. Abdulkader Tayob, *Islam: A Short Introduction* (Oxford: Oneworld Publications, 1999), 74. In the Hadith quoted (Bukhari 1.490), Tayob describes Aisha as a feminist of her time attempting to correct the secondary status given to females.

8. See also surah 5:6, which explains the cleansing process (ablution) more precisely.

9. See also Bukhari 3.84.

10. Khaled Abou El Fadl, *Speaking in God's Name: Islamic Law, Authority and Women* (Oxford: Oneworld Publications, 2001), 219, emphasis added.

11. Ergun Caner and Emir Caner, *Out of the Crescent Shadows* (Birmingham, AL: New Hope Press, 2003), 151-52. For further discussion on these "chaste women," or virgins, see Phil Parshall, *Lifting the Veil: The World of Muslim Women* (Waynesboro, GA: Gabriel Publishing, 2002), 92-5.

12. Parshall, 153.

13. Hamdun Dagher, *The Position of Women in Islam* (Villach, Austria: Light of Life, 1995), 110-12.

14. Dagher, 111.

Section Four: Women and Family

1. Hammudah Abd al-Ati, *The Family Structure in Islam* (Burr Ridge, IL: American Trust Publications, 1977), 52. Impotence, or perhaps other exceptional situations, have led some Islamic jurists to recommend chastity instead of marriage in some cases.

2. Al-Ati, 60-2.

3. Yusuf Ali, *The Holy Qur'an: English Translation of the Meanings and Commentary* (Al-Medinah, Saudi Arabia: King Fahd Holy Qur'an Printing Complex, 1410 H), 96, fn. 249.

4. Dr. Zakir Naik, "Does a Wife Have the Right to Refuse Sex with Her Husband?" www.islamicvoice.com/february.2003/religion.htm.

5. Ibn Warraq, *Why I Am Not a Muslim* (New York: Prometheus Books, 1995), 304.

6. Ergun Caner and Emir Caner, *Unveiling Islam* (Grand Rapids, MI: Kregel Publications, 2002), 137.

7. Phil Parshall *Lifting the Veil: The World of Muslim Women* (Waynesboro, GA: Gabriel Publishing, 2002), 178.

8. The repercussions of the Qur'an's allowance of wife beating are seen in contemporary societies such as Pakistan, where over 90 percent of wives have been struck, beaten, or abused sexually. See Robert Spencer, *The Politically Incorrect Guide to Islam (and the Crusades)* (Washington, DC: Regnery Publishing, 2005), 70.

9. Spencer, 73.

10. Spencer, 80.

11. Ergun Mehmet Caner, ed. *Voices Behind the Veil* (Grand Rapids, MI: Kregel Publications, 2003), 161.

12. Caner, ed., 160.

13. Of all countries, Egypt is the greatest defender of this act.

14. Muhammad, in Ahmad Ibn Hanbal 5:75, at www.light-of-life.com/eng/reveal/.

15. Material in this and the next two paragraphs adapted from www.light-of-life.com/eng/reveal/.

16. Muhammad Ibrahim Salim, *Fatwa fi khitan al-untha,* in *Liwa' al Islam,* p.330, at www.light-of-life.com/eng/reveal/.

17. Afifi Muhammad al-Saadiq, *Fi fiqh al-mar'a al-muslima* (Beirut, 1986), p.17, at www.light-of-life.com/eng/reveal/.

18. John L. Esposito, *Women in Muslim Family Law,* 2nd ed. (Syracuse, NY: Syracuse University Press, 2001), 28-34.

19. Esposito, 35.

20. Warraq, 309.

Section Five: Women and Society

1. Hamdun Dagher, *The Position of Women in Islam* (Villach, Austria: Light of Life, 1995), 113-21.

2. Ergun Mehmet Caner, ed., *Voices Behind the Veil* (Grand Rapids, MI: Kregel Publications, 2003), 105.

3. Phil Parshall, *Lifting the Veil: The World of Muslim Women* (Waynesboro, GA: Gabriel Publishing, 2002), 67.

4. "2001 Human Development Report issued by the United Nations Development Program," www .yespakistan.com/hdf/whywedoit/hdintheiw_table3.htm.

5. In percentages. The United Arab Emirates: men, 73.8; women, 78.0; Qatar: men, 80.1; women, 82.6.

6. Haifaa A. Jawad, *The Rights of Women in Islam* (New York: St. Martin's Press, 1998), 24.

7. Jawad, 21-2.

8. Nimat Hafez Barazangi, "Muslim Women's Higher Learning as a Human Right," in Mahnaz Afkhami and Erika Friedl, eds., *Muslim Women and the Politics of Participation* (Syracuse, NY: Syracuse University Press, 1997), 53.

9. Abdul Rahman al-Sheha, *Woman in the Shade of Islam* (Riyadh, Saudi Arabia: King Fahd National Library, 1421 H.), 96-8. Jawad argues for the first two of these principles as well, but defines the second principle as a job that does not "lower her dignity" (Jawad, 23).

10. For an introductory article by a Muslim on this issue, see Sheikh Abdul Azeez bin Abdullah bin Baaz, "The Danger of Women Participating in the Work Arena of Men," at www.themuslimwoman .com/herrole/dangerofwomenatwork.htm.

11. Anne Sofie Roald, *Women in Islam: The Western Experience* (New York: Routledge, 2001), 185.

12. Roald, 185.

13. Jawad notes two countries that do allow female judges: Tunisia and Malaysia (Jawad, 24).

Section Six: Women and Infidelity

1. See "Adultery" at www.answering-islam.org/Index/A/adultery.html.

2. *The Holy Qur'an: English Translation of the Meanings and Commentary,* fn 2954.

3. Adapted from Freidoune Sahebjam, *The Stoning of Soraya M.* (New York: Arcade Publishing, 1994), 119. The author demonstrates persuasively that Soraya was innocent of the charges.

4. Adapted from Sahebjam, 116-25.

5. Abdullah Saeed and Hassan Saeed, *Freedom of Religion, Apostasy and Islam* (Burlington, VT: Ashgate Publishing, 2004), 14.

6. "Death could await Christian convert," www.cnn.com/2006/WORLD/meast/03/21/afghan.chris tian/index.html.

7. See the Pact of Umar, a surrender treaty named after the second Muslim caliph. This seventh-century document disallows building, rebuilding, or remodeling churches, and it subjugates Christians and Jews, making them second-class citizens with minimal rights. See www.fordham.edu/halsall/ source/pact-umar.html.

8. Samuel Zwemer, *The Law of Apostasy in Islam* (New York: Marshall Brothers, 1924), 33.

9. Zwemer, 38.

10. Zwemer, 40-3. See also 'Abdurrahmani'l-Djaziri, *The Penalties for Apostasy in Islam* (Villach, Austria: 1997) at www.light-of-life.com/eng/ilaw/. Of the four theological schools in Sunni Islam, the Hanafi School alone rejects execution for a female apostate, while the Maliki, Hanbali, and Shafi'i schools approve it.

Section Seven: Women and Jesus

1. Ergun Mehmet Caner, ed. *Voices Behind the Veil* (Grand Rapids, MI: Kregel Publications, 2003), 27.

2. Emir Caner and Ed Pruitt, *The Costly Call* (Grand Rapids, MI: Kregel Publications, 2005), 55-6.

3. Caner and Pruitt, 106-7.

About the Authors

John Ankerberg, host of the award-winning *John Ankerberg Show,* has three earned degrees: a Master of Arts in church history and the philosophy of Christian thought, a Master of Divinity from Trinity Evangelical Divinity School, and a Doctor of Ministry from Luther Rice Seminary. He has coauthored the two-million-selling Facts On series of apologetic books, as well as *Middle East Meltdown* and *What's the Big Deal About Other Religions?*

Emir Caner was disowned by his devout Muslim father, a mosque leader, when he believed in Christ. He turned his studies toward Christian theology, earning a PhD. Recently he was selected as president of Truett-McConnell College (Cleveland, Georgia). Coauthor with his brother Ergun of the bestselling *Unveiling Islam* and numerous other books, he travels worldwide and makes many media appearances to speak about Jesus Christ.

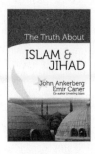